¡A TRABAJAR!
A Guide to Occupational Spanish
2nd Edition

Tara Bradley Williams

Special thanks to Jodie Parys, PhD, Jim Williams,
Maribel Borski, & Lidia Lacruz Amorós

PRONTO
SPANISH
Bridging the gap in comunication

¡A Trabajar! A Guide to Occupational Spanish
2nd Edition

ISBN: 978-1-934467-00-8

Tara Bradley Williams

Published by Pronto Spanish®, P.O. Box 92, Lake Mills, Wisconsin 53551

Table of Contents

¡Bienvenidos!

You are about to embark upon a hands-on, fun occupational Spanish conversation course that is probably unlike most courses you have taken in the past. All of our activities try to "immerse" you into real-life Spanish and push your conversational skills to the limit--whether it be with your co-workers, clients, or just for conversation in your community. It doesn't matter if you are a true beginner or someone who has taken a few previous Spanish classes, rest assured that our focus is to get you to speak and use the language and to move your Spanish skills on to the next level.

At Pronto Spanish, we do not try to inundate you with grammar rules, but rather, give you "just enough" to help you communicate—no more, no less. Throughout this series, your instructor may occasionally use a teaching method called "Total Physical Response (TPR)" and "Total Physical Response Storytelling (TPRS)" (aka "Teaching Proficiency through Reading & Storytelling"). Once you learn basic words and phrases by doing actions through TPR, you will then immediately apply these words into "stories," in order to help you get a sense of the language and its structure. This method was designed after watching babies and children acquire languages. Children do not, afterall, memorize verb charts. Rather, they learn words and grammar structures through context.

We do not strive to be "all things to all people," but rather, we focus on providing quality exercises and fun stories to help you acquire the language. If you feel like you need more grammar explanations, please go to your local bookstore or ask your instructor for recommendations on one of the many wonderful Spanish grammar books that would fit your needs.

If you have any comments or suggestions on how we can improve this course and workbook, please write us at: comments@prontospanish.com. We look forward to hearing from you!

Tips for Learning Spanish

- RELAX! Let your guard down and have some fun. Remember many Spanish-speakers and immigrants try just as hard to learn English!

- Listen for "cognates" (words that sound similar in Spanish and English). For example, "communication" is "comunicación."

- Use your face and hands to express yourself. Gesturing, pointing, and touching things all help to convey the message.

- Focus on the "big picture." Your goal is to communicate, not to understand each and every word. If you do not understand a few words (or even sentences at a time), listen for the overall message.

- Practice Spanish every chance you get. Listen to the Spanish radio and television stations, use the Spanish language or subtitle options on your DVD player, or even travel to Spanish-speaking countries. Best of all, practice with your co-workers and Spanish-speaking neighbors as much as possible.

Lección 1 - My Life

- Survival Phrases
- Greetings
- Numbers 0-9
- Pronunciation
- Job Titles

Palabras necesarias
(Survival Words)

¿Cómo se dice _____?	*KOH-moh say DEE-say*	How do you say _____?
¿Qué significa _____?	*kay sig-nif-EE-ka*	What does _____ mean?
No comprendo/No entiendo.	*no comb-PREN-doe/no ehn-TYEN-doe*	I don't understand.
No sé.	*no say*	I don't know.
Repita, por favor.	*ray-PEE-tah poor fah-BOAR*	Repeat, please.
Perdón.	*pair-DOAN*	Pardon me (for an interruption)

Saludos e introducciones
(Greetings/Introductions)

Hola
(OH-lah)

Buenos días
(BWAY-nose DEE-ahs)

¿Cómo se llama?
(KOH-moh say YAH-mah)

Buenas tardes
(BWAY-nahs TAR-days)

Me llamo _____.
(may YAH-moh)

Buenas noches
(BWAY-nahs NO-chays)

Frases de "TPR" y los cuentos
(TPR and Story Phrases)

Instrucciones: Dibuje las siguientes palabras.
Instructions: *Draw the following words.*

levántese *(lay-BAHN-tay-say)*	**hay** *(I)*
siéntese *(see-AIN-tay-say)*	**chico** *(CHEE-koh)*
camine *(kah-MEE-nay)*	**tiene** *(tee-AY-nay)*
lave *(LAH-bay)*	**le dice** *(lay DEE-say)*

Los números
(Numbers)
0-9

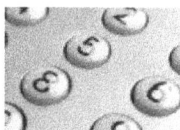

Instrucciones: Indique el número apropiado con su signo númerico.
Instructions: *Indicate the appropriate number by writing its numerical symbol.*

cero *(SAIR-oh)*	**cinco** *(SEEN-koh)*
uno *(OON-oh)*	**seis** *(sase)*
dos *(dose)*	**siete** *(see-AY-tay)*
tres *(trace)*	**ocho** *(OH-choh)*
cuatro *(KWAH-troh)*	**nueve** *(NWAY-bay)*

Matemáticas

Instrucciones: Escribe los problemas de matemáticas de tu maestro y/o pareja.
Instructions: *Write down the math problems from your instructor and/or partner.*

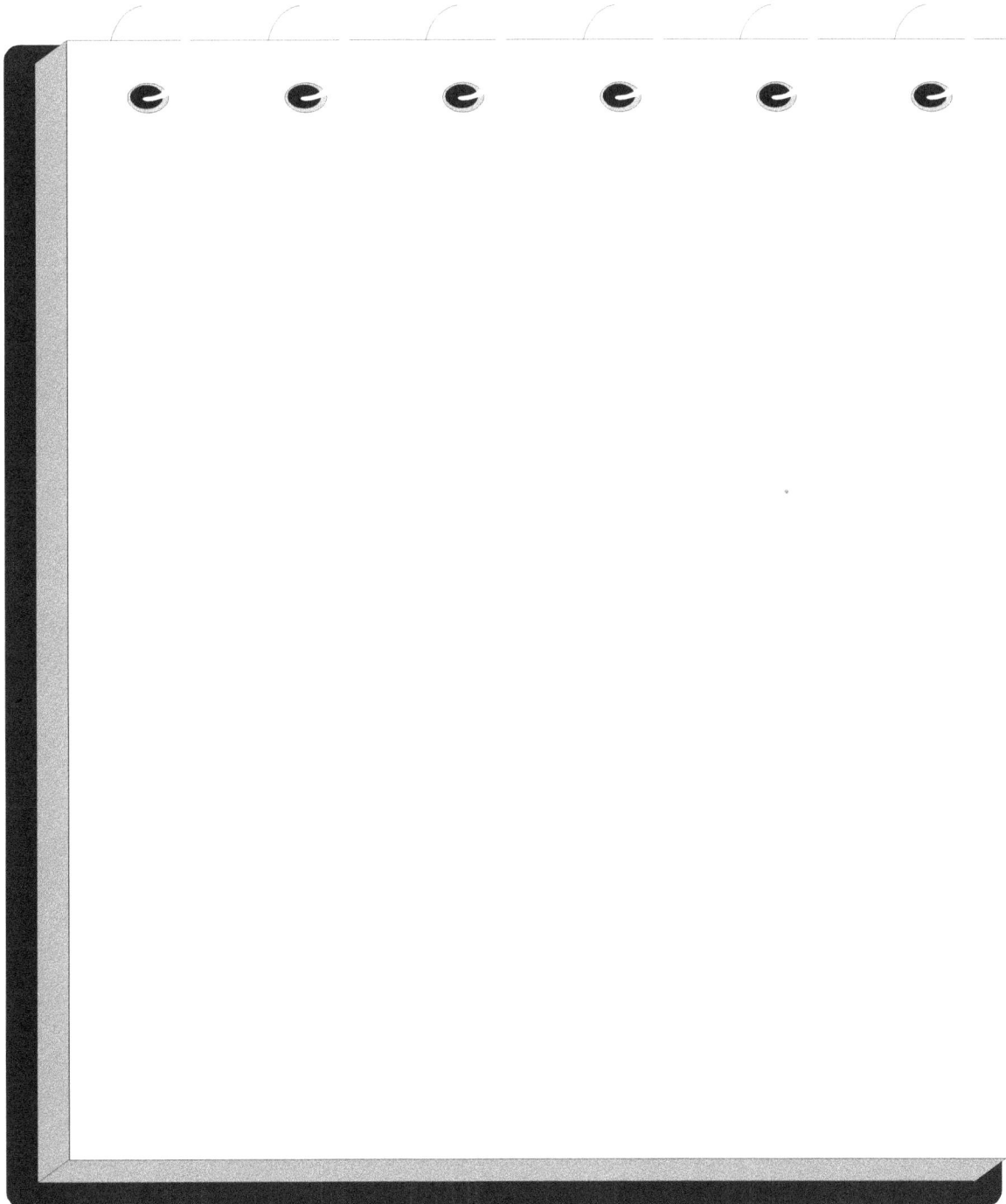

El juego: ¡A Pescar!
ah pay-SCAR
("Go Fish")

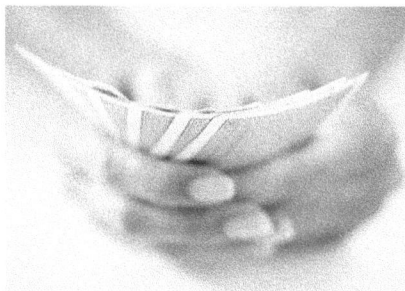

ASK:
"¿Tiene _____?" *(tee-AY-nay...)*
(Do you have ___?)

ANSWER:
"Sí, lo tengo." *(see low TANG-goh)*
(Yes, I have it.)

OR

"No, no lo tengo." *(no no low TANG-goh)*
(No, I don't have it.)

OTHER
Le toca (lay TOW-kah)	*Your turn*
Barajar (bar-ah-HAR)	*To shuffle*
Dar (dar)	*To deal*

FACE CARDS
Sota (SOH-tah)	*Jack*
Reina (RAY-nah)	*Queen*
Rey (RAY)	*King*

Pronunciación en español
(Spanish Pronunciation)

Las vocales (The Vowels)

Spanish pronunciation is actually very easy once you get the hang of it. The secret is learning the 5 vowel sounds and pronouncing them the same way each time you see the vowel.

a	(ah)	like yacht
e	(eh)	like cake
i	(ee)	like see
o	(oh)	like open
u	(oo)	like spoon

Now practice these familiar Spanish words. Remember to clearly pronounce each vowel distinctly!

a	amiga, La Bamba, salsa, cha-cha-cha
e	elefante, excelente, cerveza, tres
i	sí, gringo, Lidia, El Niño
o	ocho, no, loco, zorro, pronto
u	uno, burrito, mucho, Uruguay

13

Pronunciación de español
(Spanish Pronunciation)

Las consonantes (The Consonants)

The majority of the Spanish consonants sound the same in Spanish as in English. Here are some of the ones that may cause confusion.

c   Has 2 sounds, like in English
    1.   k sound: like "c" as in cat
        Ejemplos: coco, carro, Colorado, caliente

    2.   s sound (followed by e or i): like "c" as in celery
        Ejemplos: Celia, cine, cinco, centro

g   Has 2 sounds
    1.   g like "g" as in go
        Ejemplos: guacamole, gracias, grande, gordo

    2.   h (followed by e or i) like the "h" sound in hello
        Ejemplos: general, gente, gimnasio, gigante

h   Has no sound. Don't pronounce it.
    Ejemplos: hola, hoy, hasta, hospital

Otros(Others)

Letras	Sonido	Explicación	Ejemplos
j	h	Like hat	junio, Japón, jefe, joven
ll	y	Like yes	llamo, llave, lluvia, llorar
ñ	ny	Like canyon	mañana, señora, España, piña colada
qu	k	Like king	tequila, qué tal, queso, poquito
v	b	Like boy	vino, vista, viva, Victor
z	s	Like sat	Venezuela, Lopez, cerveza, González

Spanish Pronunciation Tips

- Try to roll your Rs for words with double Rs, "rr", or words that begin with the letter "r." (Práctica: carro, perro, rojo, rápido, ferrocarril) As an alternative, use a soft "d" sound.

- If there is an accent mark, say that section of the word with more emphasis. (Práctica: María, capitán, romántico)

- If there is no accent mark on a word and it ends in a consonant, say the last part of the word with more emphasis. (Práctica "español" and "dolor")

- If a word ends in a vowel (a, e, i, o, u), say the 2nd to last part of the word with more emphasis. (Práctica: amigo, taco, la cucaracha, enchilada)

Trabalenguas
(Tongue Twisters)

Me trajo Tajo tres trajes,
tres trajes me trajo Tajo.

Si tu gusto gustara del gusto
que gusta mi gusto,
mi gusto gustaría del gusto
que gusta tu gusto.
Pero como tu gusto
no gusta del gusto
que gusta mi gusto,
mi gusto no gusta del gusto
que gusta tu gusto.

El trapero tapa con trapos
la tripa del potro.

Como poco coco como,
poco coco compro.

El hipopótamo Hipo
está con hipo.
¿Quién le quita el hipo
al hipopótamo Hipo?

Pepe Peña
pela papa,
pica piña,
pita un pito,
pica piña,
pela papa,
Pepe Peña.

Cuca cose en casa de Coco Suca.

Work

Use this opportunity to practice your pronunciation!

Spanish	English	Spanish	English
contador/contable	*accountant*	gerente	*manager*
actor/actriz	*actor/actress*	mecánico	*mechanic*
arquitecto	*architect*	músico	*musician*
carpintero	*carpinter*	enfermero	*nurse*
cajero	*cashier*	pintor	*painter*
colega	*colleague*	plomero	*plumber*
cocinero	*cook*	oficial de policía	*police officer*
dentista	*dentist*	profesor	*professor*
doctor/médico	*doctor*	vendedor	*salesman*
electricista	*electrician*	secretario	*secretary*
ingeniero	*engineer*	cantante	*singer*
bombero	*fireman*	asistente social	*social worker*
gobernanta	*housekeeper*	maestro	*teacher*
periodista	*journalist*	técnico	*technician*
abogado	*lawyer*	camarero	*waiter/waitress*

Work & Stress

Which jobs are most stressful? Look at the following 10 occupations. In small groups, talk about the 3 most stressful jobs and 2 least stressful jobs on the list. List any others and discuss.

Trabajo	Número
vendedor	
abogado	
médico	
secretario	
madre	
maestro	
policía	
bombero	
camarero	
estudiante	

¡Utilícelo!

More Specifically...

Write in 5-10 occupations from your industry. First as individuals, rate the various occupations according to skill level & education needed. Then as a group, discuss their ratings answering "**Estoy de acuerdo**" *(ess-TOY day ah-KWAIR-doh)*, "I agree," or "**No estoy de acuerdo**" *(no ess-TOY day ah-KWAIR-doh)*, "I do not agree."

Trabajo	Número

What is your job title?

Soy...
(I am a...)

Por ejemplo:
Soy maestro. Y usted, ¿dónde trabaja?
Soy my-AY-strow. EE oo-STEHD. ¿DOAN-day trah-BAH-hah?
(I am a teacher. And you? Where do you work?)

Trabajo para XYZ Compañía. Soy ingeniero.
trah-BAH-hoh PAH-rah XYZ kohm-pahn-YEE-ah. soy een-hain-ee-AIR-oh
(I work for XYZ Company. I am an engineer.)

Notas Culturales

Nationalities & Terms

Are my co-workers and clients Hispanic? Latino? Mexican? Which phrase do I use?

The best way to refer to a Spanish-speaker is by using their nationality. If you have employees and clients from Bolivia, they are Bolivian. If they are from Mexico, they are Mexican.

The terms "Hispanic" and "Latino" are often used interchangeably and can be somewhat political. Some "Hispanics" or "Latinos" have a preference as to which term they prefer. The term "Hispanic" has become an umbrella term by the government and companies to refer to people from many different countries in Latin America and Europe. "Latinos" is more often used by the people themselves as it also refers to people from many different countries in Latin America.

So, the bottom line? Whenever possible, refer to somebody by their nationality. Otherwise, ask the people themselves if they have a preference if you use "Hispanic" or "Latino."

Lección 2 - My Time

- More Greetings
- Numbers 10-1000
- Days, Months, Date
- Time

Frases de conversación
Saludos (Greetings)

¿Cómo está? *(KOH-moh ess-TAH)* **OR** **¿Qué tal?** *(kay tahl)* (informal)	• Muy bien (++) • Bien (+) • Más o menos (0) • Así así (0) • Regular (0) • Mal (-) • Muy mal (--)	• *mwee bee-YEN* • *bee-YEN* • *mahs o MAY-nose* • *ah-SEE ah-SEE* • *ray-goo-LAR* • *mahl* • *mwee mahl*
¿Qué pasa? *(kay PAH-sah)* (informal)	• Todo bien • Nada	• *TOE-doe bee-YEN* • *NAH-dah*
¿De dónde es? *(day DOAN-day ess)*	Soy de <u>*(Puerto Rico)*</u>.	*soy day (PWAIR-toh REE-koh)*
¿Habla inglés? *(AH-blah een-GLACE)* **¿Habla español?** *(AH-blah ess-pahn-YOLE)*	• Sí (+) • Un poco *(some)* • Un poquito *(very little)* • No (-)	• *see* • *oon PO-ko* • *oon po-KEY-toe* • *No*

Los números
10-19

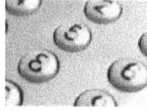

Instrucciones: Indique el número apropiado con su signo númerico.

diez *(dee-ACE)*	**quince** *(KEEN-say)*
once *(OWN-say)*	**diez y seis** *(dee-ACE ee sase)*
doce *(DOE-say)*	**diez y siete** *(dee-ACE ee see-AY-tay)*
trece *(TRAY-say)*	**diez y ocho** *(dee-ACE ee OH-cho)*
catorce *(kah-TORE-say)*	**diez y nueve** *(dee-ACE ee NWAY-bay)*

PISTA: For numbers 16-19, all you are saying is 10 plus the second number.
(16 = ten and six, "diez y seis")

Los números
20-1000

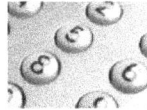

Instrucciones: Indique el número apropiado con su signo númerico.

veinte *(BAIN-tay)*	**setenta** *(say-TANE-tah)*
treinta *(TRAIN-tah)*	**ochenta** *(oh-CHAIN-tah)*
cuarenta *(kwah-RAIN-tah)*	**noventa** *(no-BANE-tah)*
cincuenta *(seen-KWEHN-tah)*	**cien / ciento*** *(see-AIN / see-AIN-toh)*
sesenta *(say-SANE-tah)*	**mil** *(meel)*

PISTA: As with the "teen" numbers, all you do is add "y" (meaning *and*) along with the second number. For example, "21" would be "veinte y uno" and "45" would be "cuarenta y cinco."

***NOTA:** "Cien" is <u>only</u> used for "100" *on the dot*. Use "ciento" for 101 and above.

Actividad – Los números de teléfono
(Telephone Numbers)

Persona A

ESCRIBIR (WRITE):

There is a party for Spanish-speaking employees at your company. Obtain the telephone numbers for the following people in order to invite them. Read the name and your partner will read you the phone number. Write the number you hear in the space provided.

¿Cuál es el número de teléfono de _____?
(kwahl ess ell NOO-mare-oh day tay-LAY-foe-no day...)

1. Sara León _____
2. Benito Guzmán _____
3. Dolores Arenas _____
4. Francisco Camacho _____
5. Tomás Jiménez _____
6. Raquel Montero _____
7. Humberto Diaz _____
8. Mariana Morales _____
9. Roberto Concejo _____
10. Marta Mesero _____
11. Ricardo Castro _____
12. Jose Marquez _____

LEER (READ):

Your partner needs the phone numbers on the following list. Be prepared to read them. (NOTE: People in Spanish-speaking countries usually pause twice when they say telephone numbers. For the number 227-3125, many would say 227-31-25 (dos, dos, siete, treinta y uno, veinte y cinco.)

El número de teléfono es _____.
(ell NOO-mare-oh day tay-LAY-foe-no ess...)

Juana Penalosa	725-1428
Lidia Cárdenas	876-6769
Gloria Ochoa	284-1321
Mateo López	725-2227
Enrique Suárez	309-2610
Pilar Hernández	722-1530
Jaime Rivas	309-2119
Alicia Mantilla	283-1825
Susana Torreón	825-1849
Alfonso Torres	863-9492
Pedro Ortiz	321-4856
Pablo Martín	286-2912

22

Actividad: Los números de teléfono
(Telephone Numbers)

Persona B

LEER (READ):

Your partner needs the phone numbers on the following list. Be prepared to read them. (NOTE: People in Spanish-speaking countries usually pause twice when they say telephone numbers. For the number 227-3125, they would say 227-31-25 (dos, dos, siete, treinta y uno, veinte y cinco.)

El número de teléfono es _____.
(ell NOO-mare-oh day tay-LAY-foe-no ess...)

Dolores Arenas	722-1930
Francisco Camacho	332-1522
Humberto Diaz	527-2817
Jose Marquez	884-4275
Tomás Jiménez	331-2016
Raquel Montero	527-2611
Mariana Morales	333-2331
Benito Guzmán	286-1327
Ricardo Castro	284-1014
Sara León	286-2412
Roberto Concejo	851-4020
Marta Mesero	451-7526

ESCRIBIR (WRITE):

There is a party for Spanish-speaking employees at your company. Obtain the telephone numbers for the following people in order to invite them. Read the name and your partner will read you the phone number. Write the number you hear in the space provided.

¿Cuál es el número de teléfono de _____?
(kwahl ess ell NOO-mare-oh day tay-LAY-foe-no day...)

1. Enrique Suárez _____
2. Mateo López _____
3. Gloria Ochoa _____
4. Pablo Martín _____
5. Juana Penalosa _____
6. Alicia Mantilla _____
7. Jaime Rivas _____
8. Pilar Hernández _____
9. Alfonso Torres _____
10. Pedro Ortiz _____
11. Lidia Cárdenas _____
12. Susana Torreón _____

Estaciones y meses del año
(Seasons and Months of the Year)

INVIERNO (een-bee-AIR-no)	PRIMAVERA (pree-mah-BARE-ah)	VERANO (bare-AH-no)	OTOÑO (oh-TONE-nyoh)
diciembre (dee-see-AIM-bray)	marzo (MAR-soh)	junio (HOO-nee-oh)	septiembre (saip-tee-AIM-bray)
enero (ay-NAIR-oh)	abril (ah-BREEL)	julio (HOO-lee-oh)	octubre (oak-TOO-bray)
febrero (fay-BRARE-oh)	mayo (MY-yoh)	agosto (ah-GO-stow)	noviembre (no-bee-AIM-bray)

PISTA:
Notice how similar the Spanish months are to the English months.

NOTA:
Much of Latin America is in the Southern Hemisphere, therefore putting the months in opposite seasons as listed above.

¡Utilícelo!

Brainstorm: What are your the busy seasons and months in your job? Why is it this time of the year?

La fecha

In most Spanish-speaking countries, the date is written with the day first, then the month, and finally the year. For example, February 10, 2003 is written 10/2/03 (NOT October 2, 2003).

Instructions: Listen to your instructor and write down the dates you hear.

FECHA
Día + Mes + Año
DEE-ah + mace + AHN-yoh

Actividad: ¿Cuándo es...?

Persona A

Start each question with:

1) Pregunte (Ask):

¿Cuándo es _____?
(KWAHN-doh ess...)

su cumpleaños   *(soo koo-play-AHN-yohs)*
la Navidad   *(la nah-bee-DAHD)*
el primer día de la primavera   *(el pree-MARE DEE-ah day la pree-mah-BARE-ah)*
su día favorito   *(soo DEE-ah fah-bore-EE-toh)*
el cumpleaños de su madre   *(el koo-play-AHN-yohs day soo MAH-dray)*
el primer día de la escuela   *(el pree-MARE DEE-ah day la ay-SKWAY-lah)*
la clase de español   *(la KLAH-say day ay-spahn-YOLE)*
Tres preguntas más:
1)
2)
3)

2) Conteste (Answer) las preguntas de la persona B.

Actividad: ¿Cuándo es...?

Persona B

1) **Conteste** (Answer) las preguntas de la persona B.

2) **Pregunte** (Ask):

¿Cuándo es _____?
(KWAHN-doh ess...)

su cumpleaños *(soo koo-play-AHN-yohs)*
la Pascua *(Easter)* *(la PAH-skwah)*
el primer día del verano *(el pree-MARE DEE-ah dell bare-AH-no)*
su día favorito *(soo DEE-ah fah-bore-EE-toh)*
el cumpleaños de su padre *(el koo-play-AHN-yohs day soo PAH-dray)*
Halloween *(hah-low-EEN)*
el día de San Valentín *(el DEE-ah day sahn bahl-ain-TEEN)*
Tres preguntas más:
1)
2)
3)

La hora
(Time)

PREGUNTA: ¿Qué hora es? (What time is it?)
kay OAR-ah ess

POSIBLES RESPUESTAS:

* For times in the 1 o'clock hour, use:
Es la una   (It is 1:00)
ess la OO-nah

Ó

Es la una y ___. (It is 1:_ _)
es la OO-nah ee ___
(Ejemplo: Es la una y veinte = 1:20)

* For all other times, use:
Son las __.   (It is _ :00)
sown lahs __
(Ejemplo: Son las tres = 3:00)

Ó

Son las ___ y ___.   (It is _ : _ _)
sown lahs ___ ee ___
(Ejemplo: Son las cuatro y diez = 4:10)

NOTA: To say "**At** what time?", you use "**¿A** qué hora?".

To answer that question, use:
"**A las ____**" (instead of "son las _____.")

Ejemplo:
PREGUNTA: ¿A qué hora es el concierto?

RESPUESTA: A las ocho.

NOTA: 24 – Hour Clock
Many Spanish-speaking countries use the 24-hour clock for travel times and appointments to avoid confusion.

Ejemplos:
13:00 = 1 pm, 18:30 = 6:30 pm

(Subtract 12 from the time to find the PM time)

Ejemplos de la hora

¿Qué hora es?

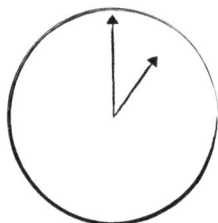

Es la una.
(ess la OO-nah)

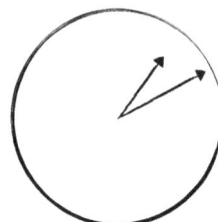

Es la una y diez.
(ess la OO-nah ee dee-ACE)

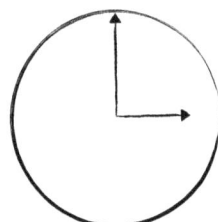

Son las tres.
(sown lahs trace)

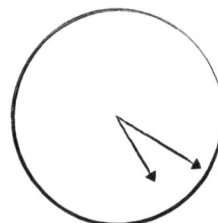

Son las cinco y veinte.
(sown lahs SEEN-koh ee BAIN-tay)

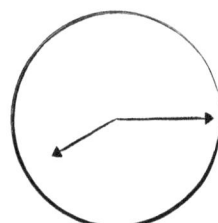

Son las ocho y quince.
(sown lahs OH-choh ee KEEN-say)

o

Son las ocho y cuarto.
(sown lahs OH-choh ee KWAR-toh)

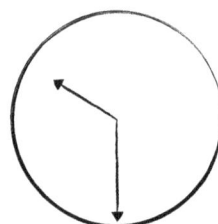

Son las diez y treinta
(sown lahs dee-ACE ee TRAIN-tah)

o

Son las diez y media.
(sown lahs dee-ACE ee MAY-dee-ah)

5:50

Son las seis menos diez.
(sown lahs sase MAY-nose dee-ACE)
It is 6 o'clock minus 10 minutes.

10:40

Son las once menos veinte.
(sown lahs OWN-say MAY-nose BAIN-tay)
It is 11 o'clock minus 20 minutes.

Otro vocabulario para decir la hora

Noon = mediodía *(may-dee-oh-DEE-ah)*   AM = de la mañana *(day la mahn-YAHN-ah)*

Midnight = medianoche *(may-dee-ah-NO-chay)*   PM = de la tarde / noche *(day la TAR-day/NO-chay)*

Los días de la semana (The Days of the Week)

Mi horario
(mee oar-AR-ee-oh)

lunes *(LOO-nays)*	martes *(MAR-tays)*	miércoles *(mee-AIR-cole-ays)*	jueves *(hoo-AY-bays)*	viernes *(bee-AIR-nays)*	sábado *(SAH-bah-doh)*	domingo *(doh-MEAN-go)*
10 am: Sr. Valdez 2 pm: Srta. Lopez	11:30 am: Sra. Vegas 2:50 pm: Sr. La Cruz 6 pm: Fútbol	8:15 am: dentista 12:00: almuerzo 3:00 pm: Srta. María Velasquez	No tengo citas.	9 am: Sr. Mendez 1:20 pm: Sra. Pelayo 4:40 pm: Sr. Garcia	FIESTA	10:30 am: Misa Descanso

ACTIVIDAD: Mi horario

Instrucciones: Haga cinco preguntas a su pareja sobre *(about)* su horario *(schedule)* de la semana. *(See the previous page.)*

Ejemplo:

Pregunta: ¿Cuándo es la cita (appointment) con el Sr. Valdez?
(KWAHN-doe ess la SEE-tah cone el sane-YORE ball-DEZ)

Respuesta: El lunes a las 10 de la mañana.
(el LOO-nays ah lahs dee-ACE day la mah-NYA-nah)

Nota:
En español la semana comienza (begins) con lunes.

Más vocabulario

hoy *(oy)*   =

ayer *(ah-YARE)*   =

mañana *(mah-NYA-nah)*   =

fin de semana *(feen day say-MAH-nah)*   =

Notas Culturales

Time

You may have noticed that Latinos and those born and raised in the United States have a very different sense of time. In the United States, "time is money." We run everything through a calendar and punctuality is key. It is considered rude to be a few minutes late.

In Latin America, people in general are much more relaxed about the clock. They feel that "what they don't get done today will keep until mañana." While this feeling may be changing somewhat among modern Latino professionals, in general, Latinos take time as it comes to allow for a natural progression of the day's events.

While it is not expected for your company to change your late policy entirely for the Latino population, you should be aware of the cultural difference and realize that the pace of life in the United States may be quite difficult to adapt to. Your Latino employees will soon realize what is expected of them if you are able to allow a bit of flexibility initially.

Lección 3 - My Environment

- Departments
- Building Areas
- Instructions

Departamentos

Instrucciones: Using the Word Bank below, write in the English department names.

Recursos Humanos	*ray-COOR-sos oo-MAH-nose*
Ventas	*BEN-tahs*
Administración	*ahd-meen-ee-strah-see-OWN*
Dirección	*dee-rek-see-OWN*
Servicio para clientes	*sair-BEE-see-oh PAH-rah klee-AIN-tays*
Producción	*pro-dook-see-OWN*
Informática	*een-form-AH-tee-kah*
Mantenimiento	*mahn-tain-ee-mee-AIN-toh*
Contabilidad	*cone-tah-bee-lee-DAHD*
Mercadeo	*mare-kah-DAY-oh*

Customer Service	Production	Administration	Information Technology	Sales
Management	Accounting	Human Resources	Maintenance	Marketing

Actividad: ¿Dónde trabaja?
(Where do you work?)

Compañía

¿Dónde trabaja (Usted)?
DOAN-day trah-BAH-hah oo-STEHD

> **Trabajo para** _____ *(compañía).*
> *trah-BAH-hoh PAH-rah* ____

¿Dónde trabaja _____ *(persona)?*
DOAN-day trah-BAH-hah

> _____ *(persona)* **trabaja para** _____ **(***compañía***).**
> _____ *trah-BAH-hah PAH-rah* _____

Por ejemplo:

¿Dónde **trabaja** (Usted)?
> **Trabajo** para Pronto Spanish.

¿Dónde **trabaja** Susana?
> Susana **trabaja** para Peakview Technologies.

Departamento

¿En qué departamento trabaja (Usted)?
en kay day-par-tah-MEHN-toh oo-STEHD

> **Trabajo en** _____ *(departamento).*
> *trah-BAH-hoh en* _____

¿En qué departamento trabaja _____ *(persona)?*
en kay day-par-tah-MEHN-toh trah-BAH-hah _____

> _____ *(persona)* **trabaja en** _____ *(departamento).*
> _____ *trah-BAH-hah en* _____

Por ejemplo:

¿En qué departamento **trabaja** (Usted)?
> **Trabajo** en Recursos Humanos.

¿En qué departamento **trabaja** Jorge?
> Jorge **trabaja** en Ventas.

Building Locations

el edificio
(el ay-dee-FEE-see-oh)

el pasillo
(el pah-SEE-yoh)

la sala de reuniones
(la SAH-lah day ray-yoon-ee-OWN-ays)

el estacionamiento
(el ess-tah-see-own-ah-mee-EHN-toh)

la entrada/la salida
(la ehn-TRAH-dah / la sah-LEE-dah)

el baño
(el BAH-nyo)

la oficina
(la oh-fee-SEE-nah)

el almacén *(storage area)*
(el ahl-mah-SEHN)

37

Direcciones (Directions)

Instrucciones: Dibuje el significado *(meaning)* de la palabra *(word)*.

a la derecha	*ah la dare-AY-cha*		debajo de	*day-BAH-hoe day*	
a la izquierda	*ah la ease-key-AIR-dah*		al lado de	*ahl LAH-doe day*	
recto/ derecho	*REK-toe/dare-AY-cho*		cerca de	*SAIR-kah day*	
detrás	*day-TRAHS day*		lejos de	*LAY-hoes day*	
delante	*day-LAHN-tay day*		aquí	*ah-KEY*	
encima de	*en-SEE-mah day*		allá	*ah-YAH*	

¿Dónde está _____? (Where is _____?)
(DOAN-day ess-TAH ____)

Español		Inglés
Vaya a _____.	*BY-yah ah*	
Siga _____.	*SEE-gah*	
Doble _____.	*DOE-blay*	
Camine _____ cuadras.	*kah-MEAN-ay ___ KWAH-drahs*	
Está _____. • muy cerca • allí • enfrente de _____. • detrás de _____. • al lado de _____. • a _____ cuadras de _____.	*Ess-TAH _____.* • *mwee SAIR-kah* • *ah-YEE* • *ain-FRAIN-tay day* • *day-TRAHS day* • *ahl LAH-doe day* • *ah ___ KWAH-drahs day ___*	

Actividad: Perdido (lost) en Milwaukee

Instrucciones: Trabaje *(work)* en parejas. Cada persona debe hacer cinco preguntas, usando el mapa que sigue.

Ejemplo:

Persona A Pregunta: Estoy en Marquette University. ¿Dónde está el Midwest Express Center?

Persona B Contesta: Está muy cerca. Siga por la avenida W. Wisconsin dos cuadras, y doble a la izquierda en la calle *(street)* N. Sixth. El Midwest Express Center está a la derecha.

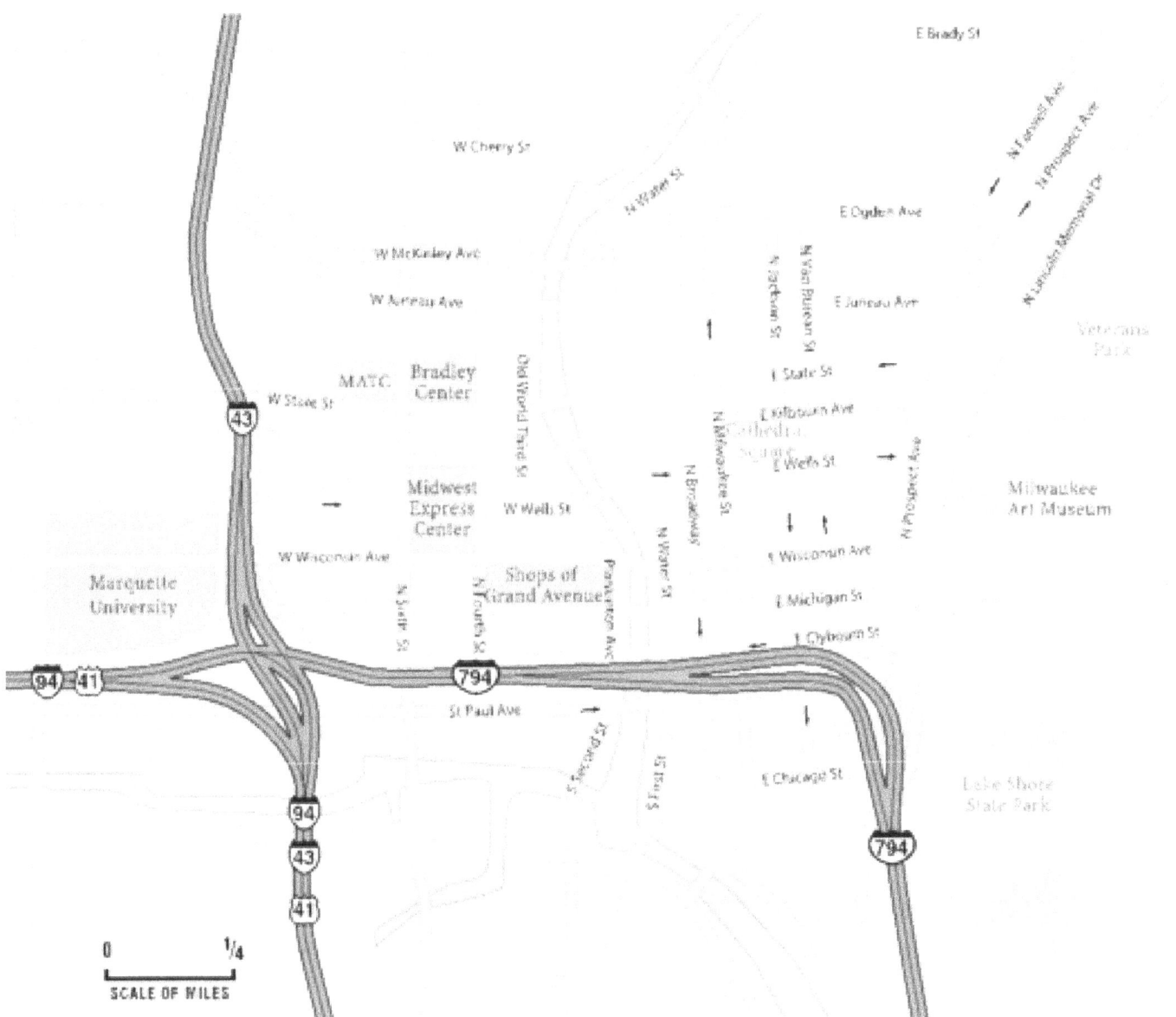

39

¡Utilícelo!

Brainstorm: List some crucial locations at your job. Draw a map and label these locations below.

Brainstorm: Where do you need to give direction to for your job? (For example: Human Resources, job site, another office building, etc.) Practice giving these directions using the map you drew above.

Notas Culturales

Work Ethic

Latinos in general have a very strong work ethic. They take pride in their work and it shows. Because of this, Latinos are often very sensitive to criticism and can be offended easily. It is not uncommon for workers to stop speaking to the person who criticized him/her or to give him/her the cold shoulder treatment. Therefore, it is important to remember that in order to correct mistakes on the job, one must first remember to praise them and build up their self-esteem first. (In fact, that is just a great management style in general!)

Lección 4 - My Job: Part I

- Equipment & Machines
- Clothing
- Colors

Máquinas

la computadora/el ordenador
*la comb-poo-tah-DOOR-ah/
el oar-den-ah-DOOR*

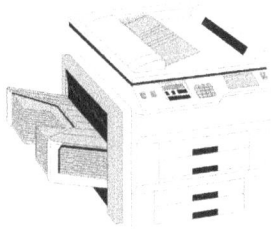

la fotocopiadora
*la foh-toh-koh-pee-ah-
DOOR-ah*

la caja registradora
*la KAH-hah
ray-hee-strah-DOOR-ah*

la cafetera
la kah-fay-TARE-ah

la calculadora
la kahl-cool-ah-DOOR-ah

el teléfono
el tay-LAY-fone-oh

el fax
el fox

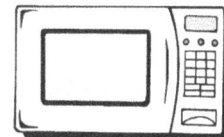

la microonda
la mee-krow-OWN-dah

"Partes" de máquinas
(Machine parts)

el botón
el bow-TONE

la tapa
la TAH-pah

las direcciones
las dee-rek-see-OWN-ays

la llave
la YAH-bay

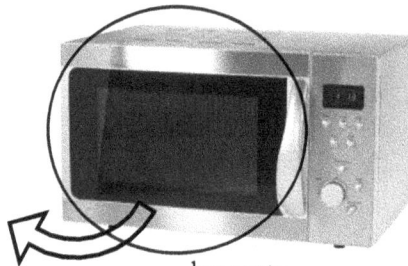

la puerta
la PWAIR-tah

el enchufe
el ain-CHOO-fay

What "parts" do you use in your job?

¡Utilícelo!

Brainstorm: What machines and tools do you use in your job? In partners, practice the following phrases and answer appropriately. (Remember to use the vocabulary most needed in your job.)

ASKING HOW TO SAY SOMETHING

Español:

¿Cómo se dice "copier" en español?
(KO-mo say DEE-say en ess-pahn-YOLE)

Inglés:

How do you say "copier" in Spanish?

ASKING WHAT SOMETHING MEANS

Español:

¿Qué significa "fotocopiadora"?
(kay sig-nif-EE-kah "foh-toh-koh-pee-ah-DOOR-ah")

Inglés:

What does "copiadora" mean?

Ropa (Clothes)

vestido
bess-TEE-doh

camisa
kah-MEE-sah

blusa
BLUE-sah

camiseta
kah-mee-SAY-tah

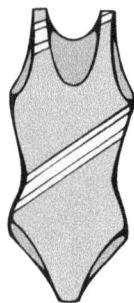

traje de baño
TRAH-hay day BAH-nyo

falda
FAHL-dah

sudadera
soo-dah-DARE-ah

chaqueta
chah-KAY-tah

pantalones
pahn-tah-LONE-ays

pantalones cortos
pahn-tah-LONE-ays CORE-tohs

suéter
SWAY-tare

zapatillas
sah-pah-TEE-yahs

zapatos
sah-PAH-toes

calcetines
kahl-say-TEE-nays

Ropa (Clothes)

aretes
ah-RAY-tays

collar
koh-YAR

anillo
ah-NEE-yoh

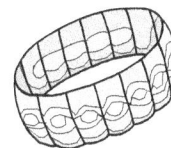

pulsera
pool-SAIR-ah

gafas/lentes
GAH-fahs/LEN-tays

gorra
GORE-ah

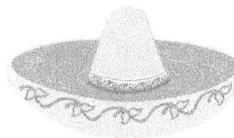

sombrero
sohm-BRAY-roh

gorro
GORE-oh

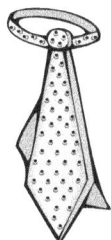

corbata
core-BAH-tah

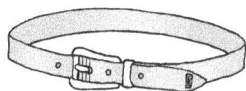

cinturón
seen-tour-OWN

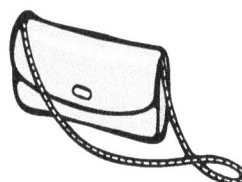

bolso
BOWL-soh

cartera
car-TARE-ah

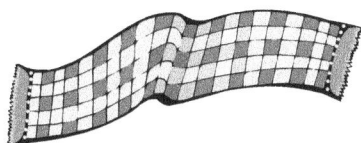

bufanda
boo-FAHN-dah

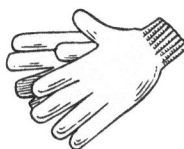

guantes
GWAHN-tays

paraguas
par-AH-gwahs

La ropa - hombre

Instrucciones: What is appropriate attire for a man at your job?
1) Tell your partner to **"dibuje un hombre que lleva..."** (draw a man that wears...)
   (dee-BOO-hay oon OME-bray kay YAY-bah...)

2) Listen to your partner and draw what he/she says.

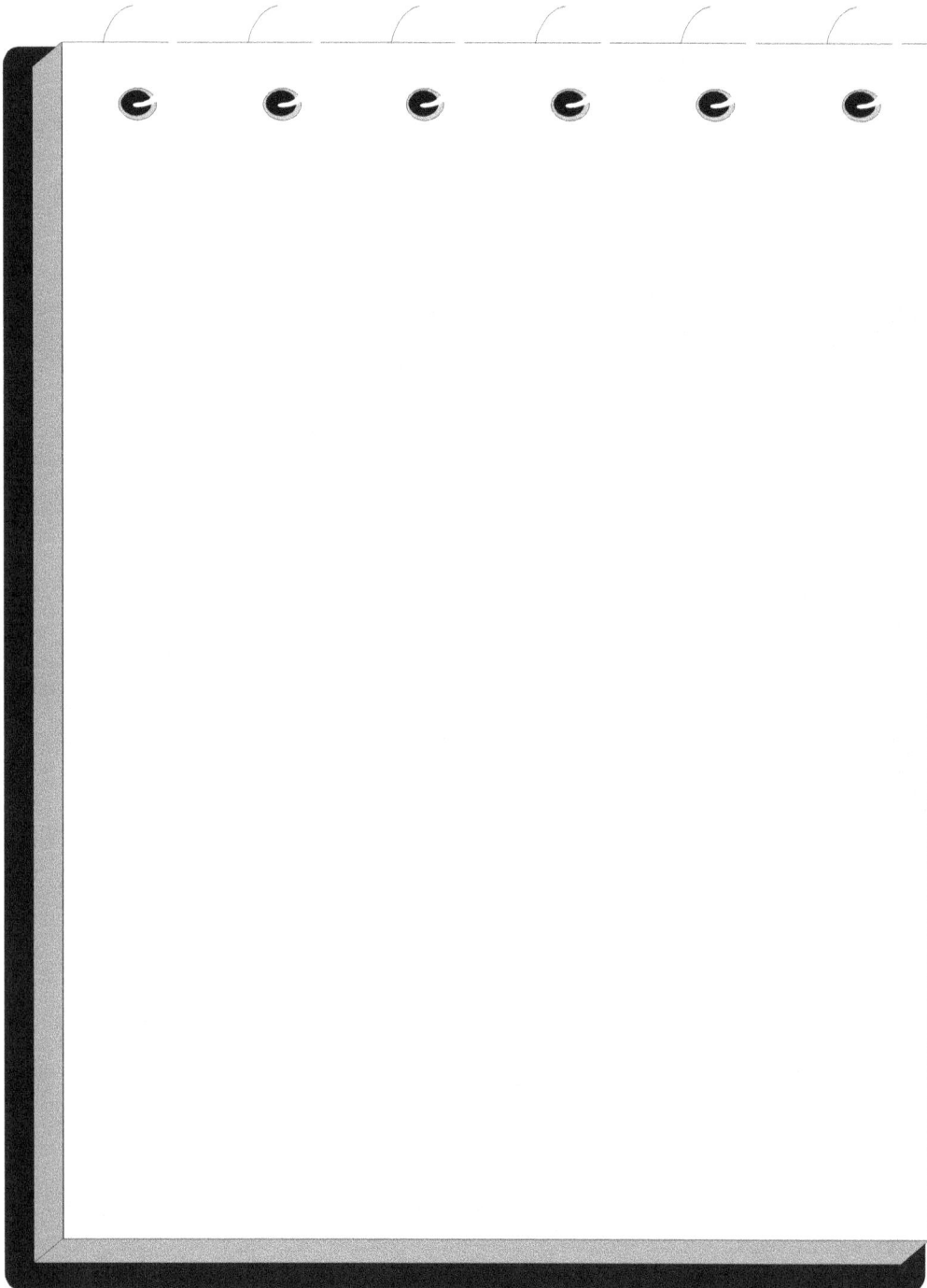

La ropa - mujer

Instrucciones: What is appropriate attire for a woman at your job?

1) Tell your partner to **"dibuje una mujer que lleva..."** (draw a woman that wears...)
   (dee-BOO-hay OO-nah MOO-hair kay YAY-bah...)

2) Listen to your partner and draw what he/she says.

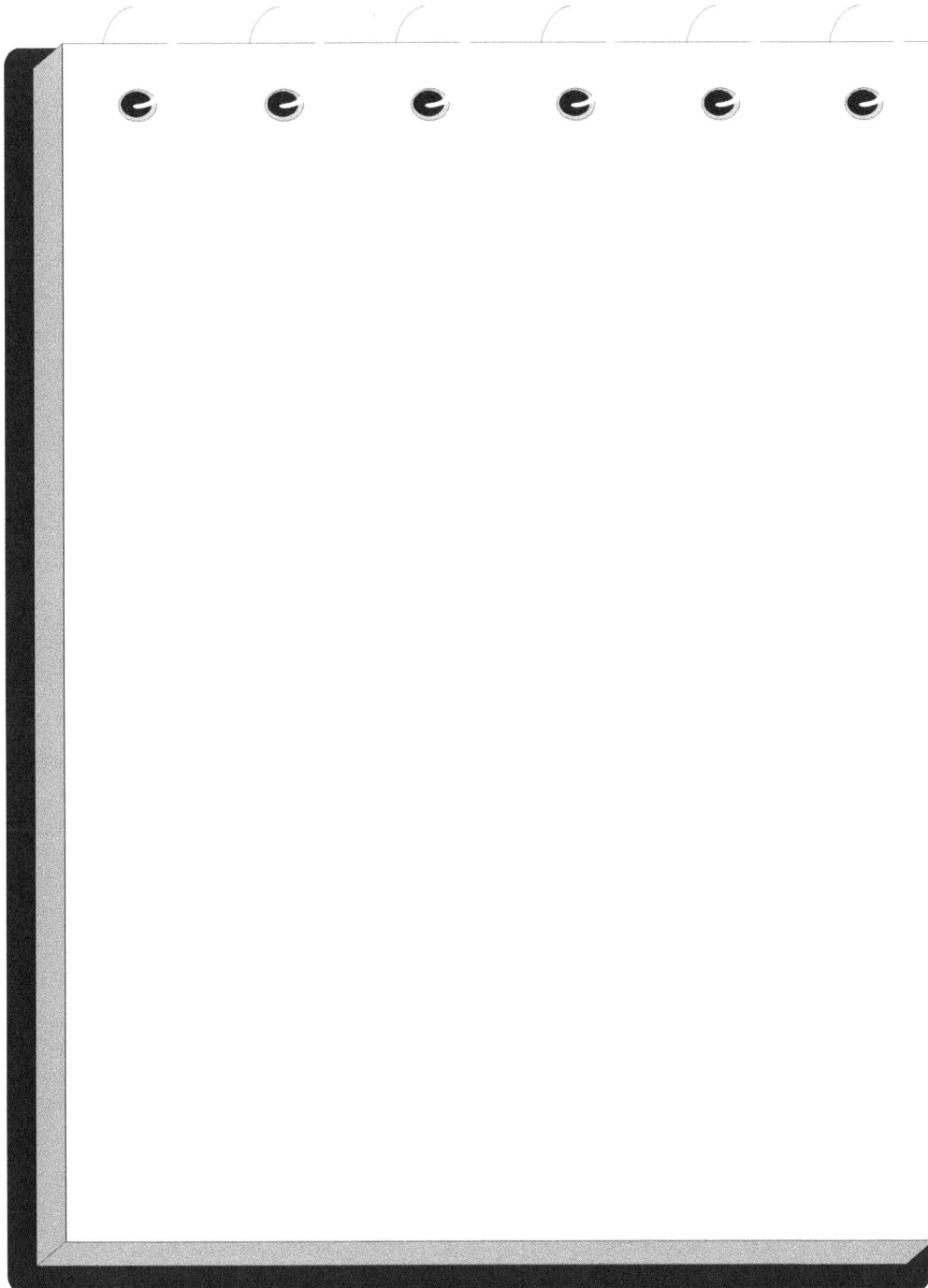

49

Los colores
(Colors)

Instrucciones: Indique el color apropriado con un creyón o lapiz de color.

rojo *ROW-hoe*	**azul** *ah-SOOL*
verde *BARE-day*	**amarillo** *ah-mar-EE-yo*
blanco *BLAHN-koh*	**negro** *NAY-grow*
morado *more-AH-doe*	**rosado** *row-SAH-doe*
naranja/anaranjado *nar-AHN-ha / ah-nar-ahn-HA-doe*	**café / pardo / marrón** *kah-FAY / PAR-doe / mar-RONE*

Actividad: BINGO de colores
(Color BINGO)

Instrucciones: Haga una tarjeta de BINGO. Coloree los cuadros con 5 colores distintos en cada columna.
Instructions: *Make your own BINGO card. Color the boxes using 5 different colors per column.*

B	I	N	G	O
		LIBRE		

B	I	N	G	O
		LIBRE		

¡Utilícelo!

Brainstorm: Why do you need colors in your job? (Some examples include a particular filing system, paint colors, "Code Red," product descriptions, etc.) Brainstorm below all the possible ways you can incorporate colors when trying to communicate with your Spanish-speaking co-workers and clients.

Notas Culturales

Hispanic/Latino Holidays

Just as we have many Holidays and hope to get the day off, so do Latinos. Below are just a few that are described. Each country is different however. Take the time to learn about the holidays that your Spanish-speaking co-workers and clients celebrate. Perhaps you can "swap" work days during important cultural events (the Superbowl versus the World Cup for example!)

Date & Origin	Celebration Name	Tradition Description
January 1 Cuba, Latin American Spain	Año Nuevo	Families attend mass and/or have dinner. The tradition is to eat 12 grapes in the seconds before the stroke of midnight, with each grape as a symbol of the last 12 months and the next 12 months to come.
January 6 Spain	Día de Los Reyes Magos	In much of Latin America, this holiday is more important than Christmas, as it is a day for the adoration of baby Jesus just like the Three Kings did when they arrived at the stable. In many countries, children get their presents on this day as opposed to Christmas day.
February 27 Dominican Republic	Dominican Republic Independence Day Carnaval	February 27th is Independence Day and the start of the Dominican Republic Carnaval. Carnaval is a four-day celebration happening from Saturday through Tuesday. Note: The date of Carnaval changes each year. (Carnaval Sunday is exactly 49 days or seven weeks before Easter Sunday.) Celebrated mainly in Brazil, Cuba, Dominican Republic, Panama, Bolivia, and Colombia.
March 21 Mexico	Birthdate of Benito Juárez	Juárez was one of Mexico's most loved presidents. He is revered for policies that assisted the poor and improved the public schools.
March/April Latin America, Spain	La Semana Santa (Holy Week)	One of the highest holy days of the year is Easter for Latino Catholics. Holy week involves solemn processions, masses, and prayer. Cascarones (confetti-filled, painted eggs) is a custom in Mexico and the U.S.
April 30 Latin America	Día de los Niños	April 30th is a holiday recognizing children as the center of the Latino family.
May 1 Latin America Spain	Dia del Trabajo	International Day of Workers. Banks, government offices, stores, post offices and businesses close for the day.

Date/Place	Name	Description
May 5 Mexico	Cinco de Mayo	Cinco de Mayo commemorates the Mexican Army of 4,500 men's victory over the 6,500 French at the Battle of Puebla in 1862. Now a celebration of Mexican food, culture, and pride.
July 6-14 Pamplona, Spain	Los Sanfermines (Running of the Bulls)	Running of the Bulls dates back to the 14th Century, but was popularized by Ernest Hemingway. Each day for a week, every day, the bulls run from old town Pamplona to the main bullfighting plaza.
September 8 Cuba	Feast of Nuestra Señora de la Caridad del Cobre	The remembrance of Cuba's patron Virgin of Charity. Cubans and Cuban Americans pray to her for inspiration and support.
September 16 Mexico	Dia de la Indepencia de Mexico	In 1810, Father Miguel Hidalgo called to his people to revolt against Spain from 300 years of Spanish rule. The war lasted for 11 years. In celebration, every year, Mexicans and Mexican Americans celebrate this day by echoing the words of Father Hidalgo, "¡Viva Mexico! ¡Viva la Independencia!"
October 12 U.S. Latin America Spain	Día de la Raza (Columbus Day)	La Raza refers to mixed race. The celebration of Columbus' arrival to the Americas is met with mixed opinion in the Hispanic/Latino culture. Some view the day as tragic based on the events to follow. Others see the day as a celebration of their mixed heritage.
November 2 Mexico, Central America	El Día de los Muertos	The holiday is centered on celebrating and honoring one's ancestors. On this day, it is said that the spirits of the dead come back for family reunions. The families honoring their dead set up altars in their homes and hold large family dinners and/or visit their loved-one's cemetery plot and decorate it with food, flowers and candles.
December 12 Mexico	Día de la Virgen de Guadalupe	The Lady of Guadalupe, which the Catholic Church named patron saint of North America, is a symbol of the marriage of European and Indian blood and beliefs. Through the years, she has also stood for cultural affirmation, political unity and freedom from oppression.
December 16-24 Mexico, Cuba, Latin America	Las Posadas	The celebration commemorates Mary and Joseph's search for a place to stay in Bethlehem. During this time, family and friends visit one another and enjoy traditional foods and singing.
December 24 & 25 Mexico, Cuba, Latin America, Spain	La Nochebuena y La Navidad	Among the holiday traditions are attending midnight mass, preparing extravagant meals, decorating the home along with lighting luminaries.

¡Utilícelo!

Brainstorm: What are the most important holidays in your culture? How do you celebrate them? How are they different from those in the Latino culture?

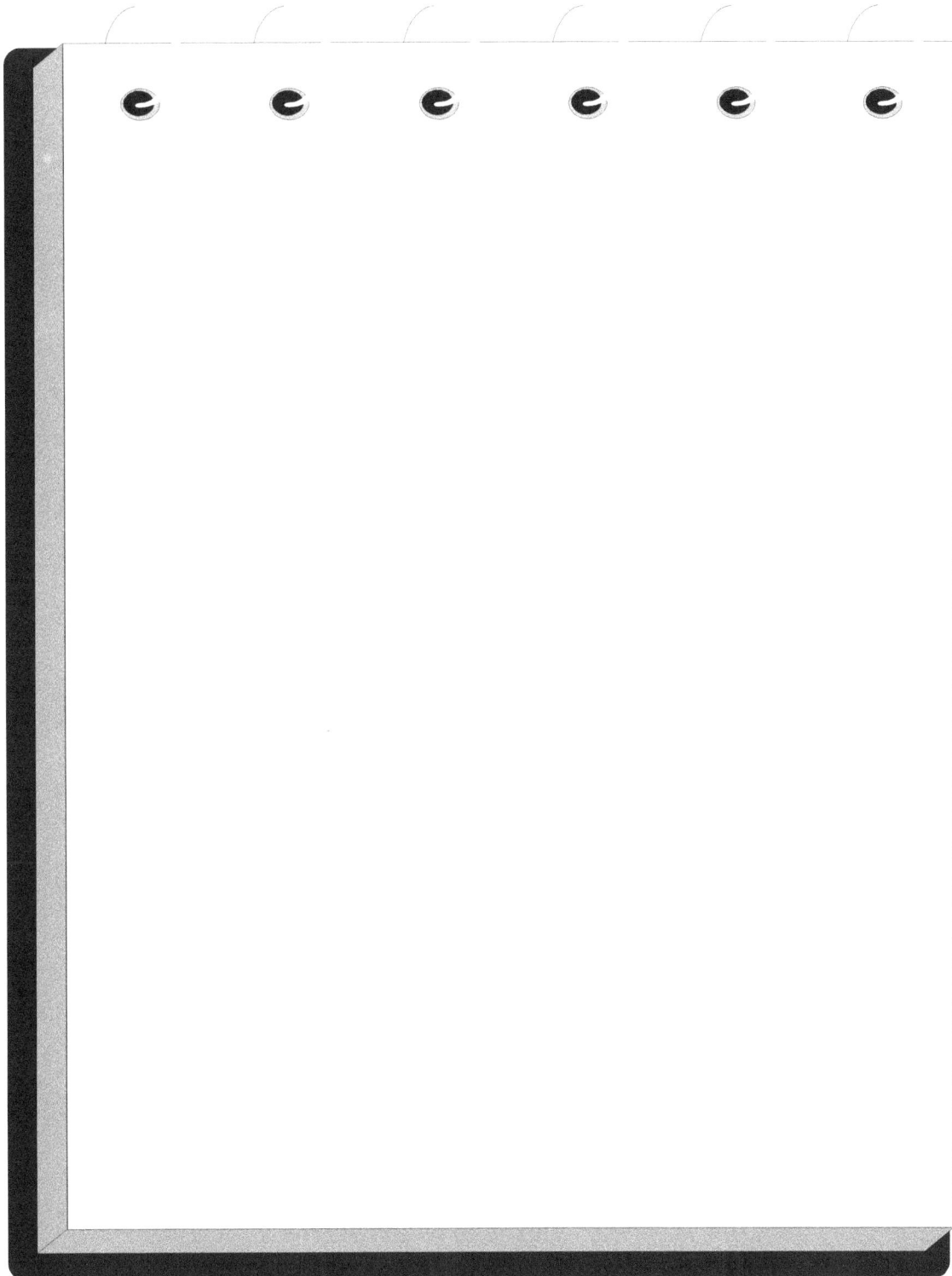

Lección 5 - My Job: Part II

- Job-Related Actions
- Supervisory Expressions
- Work Schedules

Acciones

abra
AH-brah

cierre
see-AIR-ay

llame
YAH-may

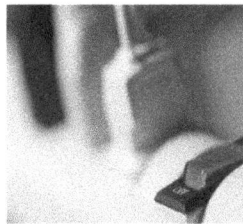

enchufe
ain-CHOO-fay

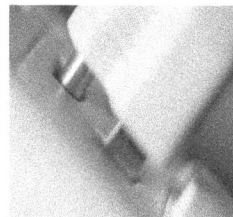

desenchufe
days-ain-CHOO-fay

apriete
ah-pree-AY-tay

haga girar
AH-gah hee-RAR

Actividad: Instrucciones

Give instructions on how to operate the machines from Lección 4.

Por ejemplo:

Fotocopiadora

Cierre la tapa. Apriete "START."
(See-AIR-ay la TAH-pah. Ah-pree-AY-tay "START.")

¡Así!

Tip: The word **"así"** comes in very handly for situations where you do not have all of the vocabulary. Basically, it means "like this" or "just like that." If you can't think of how to express something, show the Spanish-speaker how to do something, and then say **"Así."** With that one word, you are telling them to do it just like you did!

General Orders

Tráigame _____.	TRY-gah-may	Bring me _____.
Venga aquí.	BEN-gah ah-KEY	Come over here.
Venga conmigo.	BEN-gah cone-MEE-goh	Come with me.
Vaya con él.	BY-ah cone ell	Go with him.
Vaya a (la tienda).	BY-ah ah (lah tee-EHN-dah)	Go to (the store).
Ayúdeme.	ah-YOO-day-may	Help me.
Ayúdelo.	ah-YOO-day-low	Help him.
Déjelo.	DAY-hay-low	Leave it alone.
Levántelo.	lay-BAHN-tay-low	Pick it up.
Déjelo aquí.	DAY-hay-low ah-KEY	Put it down here.
Déjelo allí.	DAY-hay-low ah-YEEY	Put it down over there.
Use esto.	OO-say ESS-tow	Use this.

Instrucciones: Choose at least 5 phrases to memorize from the list and write them below. With a partner, practice the phrases and actions.

1)

2)

3)

4)

5)

¡Utilícelo!

Brainstorm: Think of at least 5 common scenarios in your job where you need to tell Spanish-speakers either 1) how to use a piece of equipment, or 2) Instructions on what they should be doing. After writing out the instructions you need, practice with others to have them follow your instructions.

Scenario 1: _____

Scenario 2 _____

Scenario 3 _____

Scenario 4 _____

Scenario 5 _____

Work Schedules

Instructions: In groups of 4, choose a 1 "Supervisor". (This person will only look at the following page.) The remaining 3 people will be "Empleados" and will stay on this page.

Empleados: Choose which "empleado" you will be (Empleado 1, Empleado 2, or Empleado 3) and give your availability to your supervisor.

★★★★★★★★★★★★★★★★★★★★★★★★★★★

Empleado #1: Puedo trabajar… *(I can work…)*
PWAY-doh trah-bah-HAR…

lunes – todo el día
martes – por las mañanas
miércoles – por las tardes
jueves - todo el día
viernes – por las noches
sábado – todo el día
domingo – no puedo trabajar

horas extras - sí
fines de semana – sólo los sábados

Empleado #2: Puedo trabajar… *(I can work…)*
PWAY-doh trah-bah-HAR…

lunes – por las mañanas
martes – por las tardes
miércoles – todo el día
jueves – no puedo trabajar
viernes – todo el día
sábado – por las noches
domingo – todo el día

horas extras - sí
fines de semana - sí

Empleado #3: Puedo trabajar… *(I can work…)*
PWAY-doh trah-bah-HAR…

lunes – por las tardes
martes – por las noches
miércoles – no puedo trabajar
jueves – por las mañanas
viernes – por las mañanas
sábado – por las tardes
domingo – todo el día

horas extras - sí
fines de semana - sí

Supervisor: Ask when employees can work and fill in the master schedule. After all spaces are filled, give them their schedule and go over it with them.

¿Puede trabajar _____ **?** *(PWAY-day trah-bah-HAR ___)*

Empleado #1: _____ (Nombre)

	Por la mañana	Por la tarde	Por la noche
lunes			
martes			
miércoles			
jueves			
viernes			
sábado			
domingo			

Empleado #1: _____ (Nombre)

	Por la mañana	Por la tarde	Por la noche
lunes			
martes			
miércoles			
jueves			
viernes			
sábado			
domingo			

Empleado #1: _____ (Nombre)

	Por la mañana	Por la tarde	Por la noche
lunes			
martes			
miércoles			
jueves			
viernes			
sábado			
domingo			

****

MASTER SCHEDULE

	Por la mañana	Por la tarde	Por la noche
lunes			
martes			
miércoles			
jueves			
viernes			
sábado			
domingo			

Notas Culturales

Communication

In the United States, "yes means yes and no means no." Supervisors say what they mean and mean what they say. Honesty and "telling it like it is" is highly regarded in our country.

This is not necessarily the case in Latino cultures. "Yes" can mean "yes, maybe, or no." Latinos tend to suggest or hint rather than coming out directly and saying what they mean. Answers are often given to avoid hurt feelings. "Saving face" and maintaining harmony are key in the Latino society. They may feel that it is not appropriate to challenge or disagree with their supervisor.

Therefore, having a good, trusting relationship with your Latino employees is key to honesty and truth. Once that bond is there, many Latinos become more open and direct with their answers.

Lección 6 - My Administration

- Basic Hiring
- Personal Characteristics & Education
- Job Application
- Telephone Calls

Basic Hiring

¿Está buscando trabajo?	*ess-TAH boo-SKAHN-doe trah-BAH-ho*	Are you looking for work?
¿Qué tipo de trabajo?	*kay TEE-poh day trah-BAH-ho*	What type of work?
¿Quiere solicitud?	*key-ARE-ay so-lee-see-TUDE*	Do you want an application?
¿Tiene transporte?	*tee-EH-nay trahn-SPORT-ay*	Do you have transportation?
¿Tiene referencias?	*tee-EH-nay ray-fair-EHN-see-ahs*	Do you have references?
Necesito ver su tarjeta de seguro social.	*nay-say-SEE-toe bare soo tar-HAY-tah day say-GOO-row so-see-AHL*	I need to see your social security card.
Necesito ver su licencia de manejar.	*nay-say-SEE-toe bare soo lee-SEHN-see-ah day mahn-ay-HAR*	I need to see your driver's license.
Necesito ver su papeles de inmigración.	*nay-say-SEE-toe bare soos pah-PELL-ays day een-mee-grah-see-OWN*	I need to see your immigration papers.
Llene esto.	*YAY-nay ESS-tow*	Fill this out.
Llámeme mañana.	*YAH-mah-may mah-NYAH-nah*	Call me tomorrow.
Regrese mañana.	*ray-GRAY-say mah-NYAH-nah*	Come back tomorrow.
(No) estamos contratando.	*(no) ess-TAH-mose cone-trah-TAHN-doe*	We (are not)/are hiring.

Brainstorm: Besides basic name and address information, list other phrases you would ask an applicant.

Características de personas – Characteristics of People

¿Cómo es? (What is he/she like?)

What are you like? From the list below, choose 5 characteristics that describe your personality. (Por ejemplo: Soy amable.) Write them under "JUEGO UNO." For JUEGO DOS, choose 5 characteristics that <u>do not</u> describe you.

With a partner, take turns asking questions (¿Es amable?) to see who is the first person to guess the other person's characteristics in JUEGO UNO. Respond to your partner's answers with the conversational responses below (Reacciones). Do the same for JUEGO DOS.

**¡No me digas!
Yo no. / Yo sí.
Yo también.
¿De verdad?**

1	2	español		inglés
____	____	alto	*AHL-toh*	
____	____	amable	*ah-MAH-blay*	
____	____	artístico	*ar-TEE-stee-koh*	
____	____	bajo	*BAH-hoe*	
____	____	bonito	*bow-NEE-toh*	
____	____	callado	*kie-AH-doh*	
____	____	cariñoso	*car-een-YOH-so*	
____	____	desordenado	*day-soar-day-NAH-doh*	
____	____	feo	*FAY-oh*	
____	____	generoso	*hane-air-OH-soh*	
____	____	guapo	*GWAH-poh*	
____	____	gracioso	*grah-see-OH-soh*	
____	____	impaciente	*eem-pah-see-EHN-tay*	
____	____	inteligente	*een-tail-ee-HEN-tay*	
____	____	joven	*HOE-ben*	
____	____	ordenado	*or-den-AH-doh*	
____	____	paciente	*pah-see-EHN-tay*	
____	____	perezoso	*pare-ee-SOH-soh*	
____	____	serio	*SAIR-ee-oh*	
____	____	simpático	*seem-PAH-tee-koh*	
____	____	sociable	*so-see-AH-blay*	
____	____	tacaño	*tah-KAHN-yoh*	
____	____	trabajador	*trah-bah-hah-DOOR*	
____	____	viejo	*bee-AY-ho*	

JUEGO UNO

Soy ... (I am..)

_____

_____

_____

_____

_____

JUEGO DOS

No soy ... (I am not..)

_____

_____

_____

_____

_____

Estudios - Studies

¿Qué estudió?
(kay ess-too-dee-OH)
What did you study?

Estudié _____.
(ess-too-dee-AY ___)
I studied _____.

contabilidad	*cone-tah-bee-lee-DAHD*	accounting	**derecho**	*dare-AY-choh*	law
publicidad	*poo-blee-see-DAHD*	advertising	**artes liberales**	*AR-tays lee-bare-AH-lays*	liberal arts
antropología	*ahn-troh-poh-low-HEE-ah*	anthropology	**lingüística**	*leen-GWEE-stee-kah*	linguistics
arte	*AR-tay*	art	**literatura**	*lee-tare-ah-TOUR-ah*	literature
astronomía	*ah-strow-no-MEE-ah*	astronomy	**matemáticas**	*mah-tee-MAH-tee-kahs*	mathematics
biología	*bee-oh-low-HEE-ah*	biology	**medicina**	*may-dee-SEE-nah*	medicine
botánica	*bow-TAHN-ee-kah*	botany	**música**	*MOO-see-kah*	music
estudios de negocio	*ess-TOO-dee-ohs day nay-GO-see-oh*	business studies	**ciencias naturales**	*see-EHN-see-ahs nah-tour-AH-lays*	natural sciences
química	*KEY-mee-kah*	chemistry	**pintura**	*peen-TOUR-ah*	painting
informática	*een-form-AH-tee-kah*	computer science	**filosofía**	*fee-low-so-FEE-sah*	philosophy
economía	*ay-kone-oh-MEE-ah*	economics	**física**	*FEE-see-kah*	physics
bellas artes	*BAY-yahs AR-tays*	fine arts	**ciencias políticas**	*see-EHN-see-ahs pole-EE-tee-kahs*	political science
idiomas extranjeros	*ee-dee-OH-mahs ex-trahn-HAIR-ohs*	foreign language	**psicología**	*see-koh-low-HEE-ah*	physicology
geografía	*hay-oh-grah-FEE-ah*	geography	**sociología**	*so-see-low-HEE-ah*	sociology
historia	*ee-STORE-ee-ah*	history	**zoología**	*so-oh-low-HEE-ah*	zoology
humanidades	*oo-mahn-ee-DAH-days*	humanities			
periodisimo	*pare-ee-oh-DEES-ee-moh*	journalism			

Más vocabulario

Obtener un título en _____	*obe-teh-NAIR oon TEE-too-low ehn*	To complete a degree in _____
Ganar dinero	*gah-NAR dee-NAIR-oh*	Earn money
Estudiar	*ess-too-dee-AR*	To study
Tomar un curso	*toe-MAR oon KOOR-soh*	To take a course

New Employee Interview

Instrucciones: You are looking for a new employee. List the characteristics that you are seeking below. Now circulate the room and do mini-interviews with the other students. Remember to do basic introductions (greetings, names, etc.)

Título de trabajo:

Características que se buscan (amable, inteligente, etc.):

5 preguntas para entrevistar:

1.

2.

3.

4.

5.

Nombre de persona	No	Posible	Sí

¿Quién es su empleado nuevo? ¿Por qué?

Actividad: Información del cliente

You have now learned almost everything you need to take down general information on a Spanish-speaking client. You may, however, still be nervous about not understanding yout client or knowing how to spell in Spanish. We could spend time on learning the Spanish alphabet, but this is often a very time consuming project. It is much easier and more time effective to learn these three words:

¿Cómo se escribe?
(KOH-moh say ay-SKREE-bay)
How is it written?

For example, if you ask for the patient's name, and he rattles off, "Juan Luis Gutiérrez Martínez," simply ask the three magic words, giving him a pencil and paper and copy what he writes.

ESCRIBIR:

You work at an employment agency and are helping the Spanish-speakers fill out their applications. Ask your partner the following information.

Start each question with:

¿Cuál es su _____?
(KWAHL ess soo _____)

Nombre: _____

nome-bray

Dirección: _____

dee-rek-see-OWN

Ciudad: _____ **Estado:** _____ **Zona Postal:** _____

see-oo-DAHD   *ess-TAH-doh*   *SO-nah poh-STAHL*

Número de teléfono: _____

NOO-mare-oh day tay-LAY-fo-no

Número de celular: _____

NOO-mare-oh day say-loo-LAR

Dirección de correo electrónico: _____

dee-rex-see-OWN day core-AY-oh ay-lake-TRAHN-ee-koh

Fecha de nacimiento (birth): _____ **Edad (age):** _____

FAY-cha day nah-see-mee-EN-toe   *ay-DAHD*

Lugar (place) de nacimiento: _____

loo-GAR day nah-see-mee-EN-toe

Nacionalidad: _____ **Sexo:** _____

nah-see-oh-nahl-ee-DAHD   *SEX-oh*

Número de seguro social: _____

NOO-mare-oh day say-GOO-row so-see-AHL

Llamadas telefónicas – Telephone Calls
Here is an opportunity to practice your pronunciation in these next exercises!

HACER UNA CITA

EXAMPLE *(making an appointment with the receptionist)*

María Bañuelos
Appointment with Tomás
Wednesday, May 10
2:30 pm

RECEPCIONISTA:
¿Bueno?

CLIENTE:
Buenos días. **Me gustaría hacer una cita** con Tomás.

RECEPCIONISTA:
¿De parte de quién?

CLIENTE:
Me llamo María Bañuelos.

RECEPCIONISTA:
¿Cuándo **le gustaría hacer la cita**?

CLIENTE:
El miércoles, el 10 de mayo.

RECEPCIONISTA:
¿Está disponible a las 2 y media de la tarde?

CLIENTE:
Sí. Está bien.

RECEPCIONISTA:
Muy bien. ¡Hasta el miércoles!

CLIENTE:
Adiós.

ACTIVIDAD:
Make an appointment with the following information.
Maricela Martinez
Appointment with Natalia
Thursday, May 11 at 8:30 am

Llamadas telefónicas – Telephone Calls

DEJAR UN MENSAJE

EXAMPLE

(leaving a message with the receptionist)

María Bañuelos
Leaving a message for Jaime
Phone: 608-256-3985

RECEPCIONISTA:
¿Bueno?

CLIENTE:
Buenas tardes. ¿Está Jaime?

RECEPCIONISTA:
No, no está. ¿Quiere dejar un mensaje?

CLIENTE:
Sí. Me llamo María Bañuelos. **Quiero hacer una cita** con Jaime.

RECEPCIONISTA:
¿Cuál es su número de teléfono?

CLIENTE:
Mi número de teléfono es 608-256-3985.

RECEPCIONISTA:
Gracias. **Le voy a dar el mensaje** a Jaime.

CLIENTE:
Gracias. Adiós.

RECEPCIONISTA:
Adiós.

ACTIVIDAD:

Leave a message with the following information.

Maricela Martinez
Leaving a message for Daniela
Phone: 712-289-4813

71

HACER UNA CITA

EXAMPLE
(receptionist answers and transfers call to make the appointment)

María Bañuelos
Appointment with Mercedes
Wednesday, October 25
2:30 pm

RECEPCIONISTA:
¿Bueno?

CLIENTE:
Buenos días. **¿Está Mercedes?**

RECEPCIONISTA:
Sí. Un momento.

MERCEDES:
Hola. **Soy Mercedes.**

CLIENTE:
Hola Mercedes. Me llamo Maria Bañuelos. **Quiero hacer una cita con Usted.**

MERCEDES:
¿Cuándo **le gustaría hacer la cita**?

CLIENTE:
El miércoles, el 25 de octubre.

MERCEDES:
¿Está disponible a las 2 y media de la tarde?

CLIENTE:
Sí. Está bien.

MERCEDES:
Muy bien. ¡Hasta el miércoles!

CLIENTE:
Adiós.

ACTIVIDAD:
Make an appointment with the following information.
Maricela Martinez
Appointment with Rosario, Thursday, October 26 at 8:30 am

Dejar y escribir mensajes
(Leaving and Taking Messages)

Instructions: Give the following messages to your partner or make the appropriate appointments. Then listen to your partner as she gives you her messages and write them down on the following page.

Persona A

Make an appointment with Juana on Monday, May 12 at 3:00 pm.	Make an appointment with Beatriz on Tuesday, June 3 at 11:00 am.
Leave a message for Ana. You want to make an appointment on Tuesday, April 13 at 4:30 pm.	Leave a message for Susana. You want to make an appointment on Wednesday, September 13 at 12:00 noon.
Ask to talk to Cecilia. When she is on the phone, make an appointment on Friday, January 16 at 10:30 am.	Ask to talk to Teresa. When she is on the phone, make an appointment Thursday, July 20 at 1:45.

Persona B

Make an appointment with Guillermo on Monday, February 15 at 4:00 pm.	Make an appointment with Rosario on Tuesday, October 9 at 8:00 am.
Leave a message for Roberto. You want to make an appointment on Tuesday, July 28 at 2:30 pm.	Leave a message for Federico. You want to make an appointment on Wednesday, March 17 at 12:30.
Ask to talk to Jaime. When he is on the phone, make an appointment on Friday, August 30 at 10:00 am.	Ask to talk to Adán. When he is on the phone, make an appointment Thursday, December 21 at 11:45.

MENSAJES

Fecha y hora:
Para:
De parte de quién:
Mensaje:

Fecha y hora:
Para:
De parte de quién:
Mensaje:

Fecha y hora:
Para:
De parte de quién:
Mensaje:

Fecha y hora:
Para:
De parte de quién:
Mensaje:

Fecha y hora:
Para:
De parte de quién:
Mensaje:

Fecha y hora:
Para:
De parte de quién:
Mensaje:

Notas Culturales

Understanding the Naming System

Many people from Latin America and Spain use a different naming system than the traditional U.S. system, which is:

First Name, Middle Name, Last Name
(U.S. women often change their last name when they get married)

In many Latin American countries, they use:

First Name, 1st/Father's Last Name, 2nd/Mother's Last Name

For example, if you meet **Juan Martínez Gomez**, his first name is Juan, and:

Martínez is Juan's **father's last name** (NOT his middle name)
Gomez is Juan's **mother's last name**

If **Juan Martínez Gomez** marries **Ana Hernandez Lopez***, their child would be named:

Lupe Martínez Hernandez (the father's name is always carried down).

In some countries, the woman's name would never change...even if she got married! In others, some women may drop their 2nd last name and take on the name of their husband. For example, Ana may become Ana Hernandez de Martínez.

With common sounding U.S. names, let's say **John Smith** marries **Susan Jones**. They both keep their names. If they have a son, his name would become Bobby Smith Jones.

Let's try it with your name.

What is your father's name? First name _____ Last Name _____
What is your mother's name? First name _____ Maiden Name _____

Using the Latino naming system, what would your name be?

_____

First Name   Middle Name   Father's Last Name   Mother's Maiden Name

Lección 7 - My Employees & Relationships

- Rules & Expectations
- Family
- Likes/Dislikes

Reglas
(Rules)

Prohibido comer.	Prohibido fumar.	Prohibido beber.
pro-hee-BEE-doh koh-MARE	*pro-hee-BEE-doh foo-MAR*	*pro-hee-BEE-doh bay-BARE*

No use drogas.	*no OO-say DROH-gahs*	Don't use drugs.
Estacione al frente/atrás.	*ess-tah-see-OWN-ay ahl FREHN-tay/ ah-TRAHS*	Park in front/back.
Estacione allá.	*ess-tah-see-OWN-ay ah-YA*	Park over there.
Use la entrada de empleados.	*OO-say la en-TRAH-dah day ehm-play-AH-dose*	Use the employee entrance.
Prohibido el acoso sexual.	*pro-hee-BEE-doh ah-KOH-soh sex-WAHL*	No sexual harassment.
Prohibidos los chistes o fotos groseras.	*pro-hee-BEE-doe los CHEE-stays oh FOE-toes grow-SAIR-ohs*	No dirty jokes or pictures.

Esperanzas del trabajo
(Job Expectations)

Tiene que...
tee-AY-nay kay
(You have to...)

ó

Necesita....
nay-say-SEE-tah
(You need to...)

avisarme si no entiende algo	*ah-bee-SAR-may see no ehn-tee-EHN-day AHL-goh*	tell me if you do not understand something
avisarme si tiene un problema	*ah-bee-SAR-may see tee-EHN-ay oon pro-BLAY-mah*	tell me if you have a problem
estar muy limpio	*ess-TAH mwee LEEM-pee-oh*	be very clean
hacer un buen trabjo	*ah-SAIR oon bwehn trah-BAH-ho*	do a good job
llamar si no puede venir al trabajo	*yah-MAR see no PWAY-day ben-EER ahl trah-BAH-ho*	call if you cannot come to work
mantener la ropa limpia	*mahn-tehn-AIR la ROW-pah LEEM-pee-ah*	have clean clothes
mantener el uniforme limpio	*mahn-tehn-AIR el oon-ee-FORM-ay LEEM-pee-oh*	have a clean uniform
ser amable en el trabajo	*sair ah-MAH-blay en ehl trah-BAH-ho*	be friendly at work
ser cortés a los clientes	*sair core-TAYS ah los klee-AIN-tays*	be courteous to customers

List others that apply to your job:

¿Cómo estoy haciendo en mi trabajo?

KOH-moh ess-TOY ah-see-AIN-doh ehn mee trah-BAH-hoh

(How am I doing in my job?)

Positivo ✚	Negativo ▬	inglés
Hace un buen trabajo.	No hace un buen trabajo	You are/are not doing a good job.
AH-say oon bwen trah-BAH-ho	*no AH-say oon bwen trah-BAH-ho*	
Estamos satisfechos.	No estamos satisfechos.	We are/are not satisfied.
ess-TAH-mose saht-ees-FAY-chos	*no ess-TAH-mose saht-ees-FAY-chos*	
Su jefe está satisfecho.	Su jefe no está satisfecho.	You boss is/is not pleased.
soo HAY-fay ess-TAH saht-ees-FAY-cho	*soo HAY-fay no ess-TAH saht-ees-FAY-cho*	
Su rendimiento es satisfactorio.	Su rendimiento no es satisfactorio.	Your performance is/is not satisfactory.
soo rain-dee-mee-EN-toe ess saht-ees-fahk-TAR-ee-oh	*soo rain-dee-mee-EN-toe no ess saht-ees-fahk-TAR-ee-oh*	

List others that apply to your job:

Quejas

KAY-hahs
(Complaints)

Hay una queja de Usted sobre...
I OO-nah KAY-hah day oo-STEHD SO-bray
(There's a complaint about you for...)

abuso de alcohol	*ah-BOO-soh day ahl-KOHL*	alcohol abuse
abuso de drogras	*ah-BOO-soh day DROW-gahs*	drug abuse
acoso sexual	*ah-KOH-soh sex-WAHL*	sexual harassment
falta al trabajo	*FAHL-tah ahl trah-BAH-hoh*	missing work
falta de ayuda a su supervisor	*FAHL-tah day ah-YOO-dah ah soo soo-pare-bee-SOAR*	not helping your supervisor
falta de buena actitud	*FAHL-tah day BWEN-ah ahk-tee-TOOD*	poor attitude
llegar retrasado	*yay-GAR ray-tray-SAH-doh*	arriving late
no llevarse bien con los otros empleados	*no yay-BAR-say byen cone los OH-trow ehm-play-AH-dohs*	not getting along with other employees
trabajo de poca calidad	*trah-BAH-hoh day POH-koh kah-lee-DAHD*	poor work quality

List others that apply to your job:

Avisos y despedidas

ah-BEE-sohs ee day-spay-DEE-dahs
(Warnings & Dismissals)

Ésta es una llamada de atención verbal.	*ESS-tah ess OO-nah yah-MAH-dah day ah-ten-see-OWN bare-BAHL*	This is a verbal warning.
Ésta es una llamada de atención por escrito.	*ESS-tah ess OO-nah yah-MAH-dah day ah-ten-see-OWN poor ess-KREE-toh*	This is a written warning.
Esto es serio.	*ESS-tow ess SAIR-ee-oh*	This is serious.
Usted estará despedido si esto continúa.	*oo-STEHD ess-tar-AH day-spay-DEE-doh see ESS-tow cone-tee-NEW-ah*	You will be fired if this continues.
Usted está despedido.	*oo-STEHD ess-TAH day-spay-DEE-doh*	You are fired.

List others that apply to your job:

80

¡Utilícelo!

You are responsible for annual performance reviews for 2 of your employees. In groups of 3, take turns interviewing and having a discussion around their job performance.

Nombre: _____

	Sí	No	A veces (sometimes)
Hace un buen trabajo.			
Hay quejas del empleado			
Llega retrasado			
Se lleva bien con los otros empleados			
Se lleva bien con su supervisor			
Trabajo es de buena calidad			
Otro:			

Comentarios:

¡Utilícelo!

Nombre: _____

	Sí	**No**	**A veces (sometimes)**
Hace un buen trabajo.			
Hay quejas del empleado			
Llega retrasado			
Se lleva bien con los otros empleados			
Se lleva bien con su supervisor			
Trabajo es de buena calidad			
Otro:			

Comentarios:

La familia – Mis parientes

la fah-MEE-lee-ah - mees pah-ree-AIN-tays
(The Family – My Relatives)

Juan   Lidia

Silvia   Roberto

Juana   David

José   Rosa

María   Santi   Susana

abuelo/a	*ah-BWAY-loh/lah*	grandfather/ grandmother	**sobrino/a**	*so-BREE-noh/nah*	nephew/niece
padre	*PAH-dray*	father	**esposo/a**	*ess-POH-soh/sah*	spouse
madre	*MAH-dray*	mother	**padrino/madrina**	*pah-DREE-noh/ mah-DREE-nah*	godfather/ godmother
hijo/a	*EE-hoh/hah*	son/daughter	**parientes**	*pah-ree-AIN-tays*	relatives
hermano/a	*air-MAH-noh/nah*	brother/sister	**padrastro**	*pah-DRAH-stroh*	step-father
nieto/a	*nee-ATE-oh/ah*	grandson/ granddaughter	**madrastra**	*mah-DRAH-strah*	step-mother
tío/a	*TEE-oh/ah*	uncle/aunt	**hijastro/a**	*ee-HAH-stroh/strah*	step-son/ daughter
primo/a	*PREE-moh/mah*	cousin	**hermanastro/a**	*air-mahn-AH-stroh/ strah*	step-brother/ sister

Instructions: Practice asking who people are in the family, using "¿Quién es _____?" (Who is _____?).
Ejemplos:

¿Quién es el hermano de Susana?   *(KEY-ain ess el air-MAH-noh day soo-SAH-nah)*
¿Quién es el sobrino de Juana?   *(KEY-ain ess el so-BREE-noh day HWAH-nah)*
¿Quién es el hijo de Juan?   *(KEY-ain ess el EE-hoh day hwahn)*

83

Actividad: Árbol de la familia

Instructions: Draw your own family tree in the space provided, labeling each family member with a Spanish word. When finished, ask your partner the following questions about his/her family. Be prepared to answer the same questions regarding your family.

PREGUNTAS:

1. ¿Cómo se llama su madre?
2. ¿Tiene *(do you have)* hijos? ¿Cuántos? *(How many?)*
3. ¿Tiene hermanos? ¿Cómo se llaman?
4. ¿Cómo se llaman sus abuelos?
5. Ask at least 5 more questions pertaining to your partner's family.

Frases de conversación con "gustar"
(Likes / Dislikes)

It is easy to make basic conversation by asking people what they like and do not like. Your Spanish-speaking co-workers and neighbors can also get to know you better this way as well!

To ask someone if they **LIKE** something, say:

PREGUNTA (QUESTION):

¿Le gusta _____ ?
lay GOO-stah

RESPUESTA (ANSWER):

Sí, me gusta _____.
see may GOO-stah
(Yes, I like ___.)

OR

No, no me gusta ____.
no no may GOO-stah
(No, I do not like___.)

To ask someone what they like **TO DO**, say:

PREGUNTA (QUESTION):

¿Qué le gusta hacer?
kay lay GOO-stah ah-SAIR

(HACER means "TO DO".)

RESPUESTA (ANSWER):

Me gusta _____.
may GOO-stah _____

Actividades posibles

leer	*lay-AIR*	read	mirar la televisión	*meer-AR la tell-ee-bee-see-OWN*	watch tv
comer	*koh-MARE*	eat	ir al cine	*eer ahl SEE-nay*	go to the movies
jugar al /	*hoo-GAR ahl /*	play /	tocar el piano	*tow-CAR el pee-AH-noh*	play piano
mirar el	*meer-AR ahl*	watch	trabajar en el jardín	*trah-bah-HAR en el har-DEEN*	work in the garden
• baloncesto	• *bah-lone-SESS-tow*	• basketball	estar con mi familia	*ess-TAR cone mee fah-MEE-lee-ah*	be with my family
• golf	• *golfe*	• golf	hacer ejercicio	*ah-SAIR ay-hair-SEE-see-oh*	exercise
• béisbol	• *BAYS-bole*	• baseball			
• fútbol	• *FOOT-bole*	• soccer	viajar	*bee-ah-HAR*	travel
• fútbol americano	• *FOOT-bole ah-mare-ee-KAH-noh*	• football	cocinar	*koh-see-NAR*	cook
• tenis	• *TEH-nees*	• tennis	estar con amigos	*ess-TAR cone ah-MEE-gohs*	spend time with friends

Actividad: Entrevista de intereses
(Interest Survey)

Instructions: Go around the room and ask people what they like to do. When someone likes an activity, have him/her initial the appropriate box. (Maximum 2 boxes per person.)

PREGUNTA: ¿Le gusta _____?

RESPUESTA: Me gusta _____ OR No, no me gusta _____.

Jugar al golf	Escuchar música	Comer	Mirar fútbol americano
Viajar	Cocinar	Leer	Trabajar en el jardín.
Estar solo	Jugar al baloncesto	Tocar un instrumento	Ir al cine
Jugar con computadoras	Trabajar	Escribir	Estar con tu (mi) familia

Notas Culturales

Family

In the United States, family means many different things to many different people. It is not uncommon to have parents and siblings spread all across the country and only get together every few years. We often refer to our family as just the parents and children. Due to societal factors such as both parents working full-time, single parents raising children, and families spread out among large distances, children in the United States are encouraged to become independent thinkers early on. Therefore, many employees in the United States look forward to positions with more responsibility and seek to "climb the corporate ladder."

In the Latino culture, the family is central. It is the strength of the Latino society. The "immediate" family often includes parents, children, cousins, grandparents, aunts, uncles, etc. Weekend entertainment many times include all of these people on a regular basis.

In a traditional Latino family, the father is the decision maker and often, the mother is more subordinate. She is a valued and devoted wife and mother. Because of this traditional family structure, most Latinos do not have a problem with undisputed authority. They may even seem submissive to their supervisor and unquestioningly, accept instructions. It may also be seen that they are content with their positions and are not actively seeking promotions and positions with greater leadership. As co-workers, be mindful of these cultural differences. If you see leadership potential, nurture it!

Lección 8 - My Safety & Health

- Body Parts
- Emergencies, Accidents & Injuries
- Safety Equipment

Las partes del cuerpo
(The Parts of the Body)

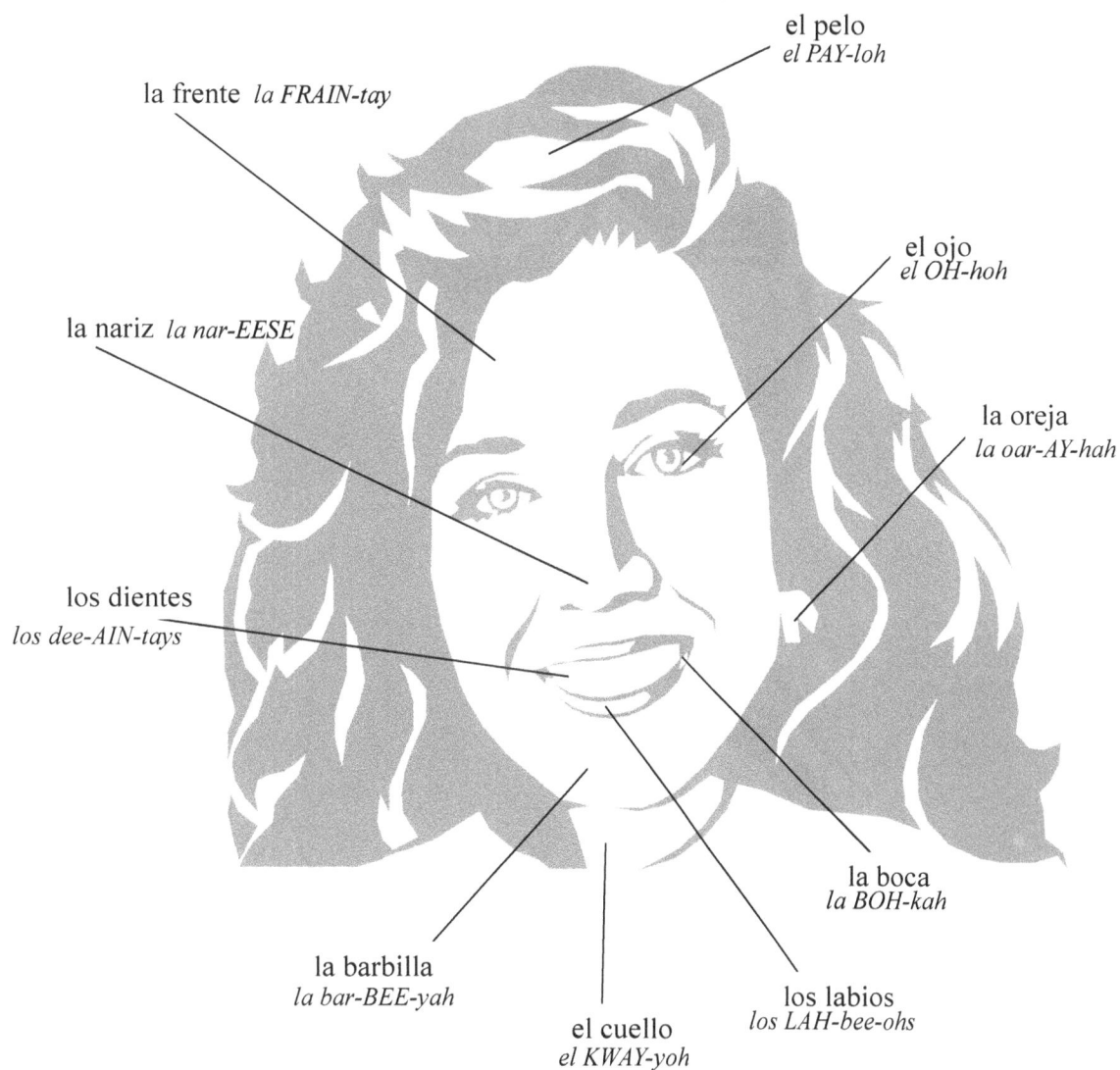

el pelo
el PAY-loh

la frente *la FRAIN-tay*

el ojo
el OH-hoh

la nariz *la nar-EESE*

la oreja
la oar-AY-hah

los dientes
los dee-AIN-tays

la boca
la BOH-kah

la barbilla
la bar-BEE-yah

el cuello
el KWAY-yoh

los labios
los LAH-bee-ohs

89

Las partes del cuerpo
(The Parts of the Body)

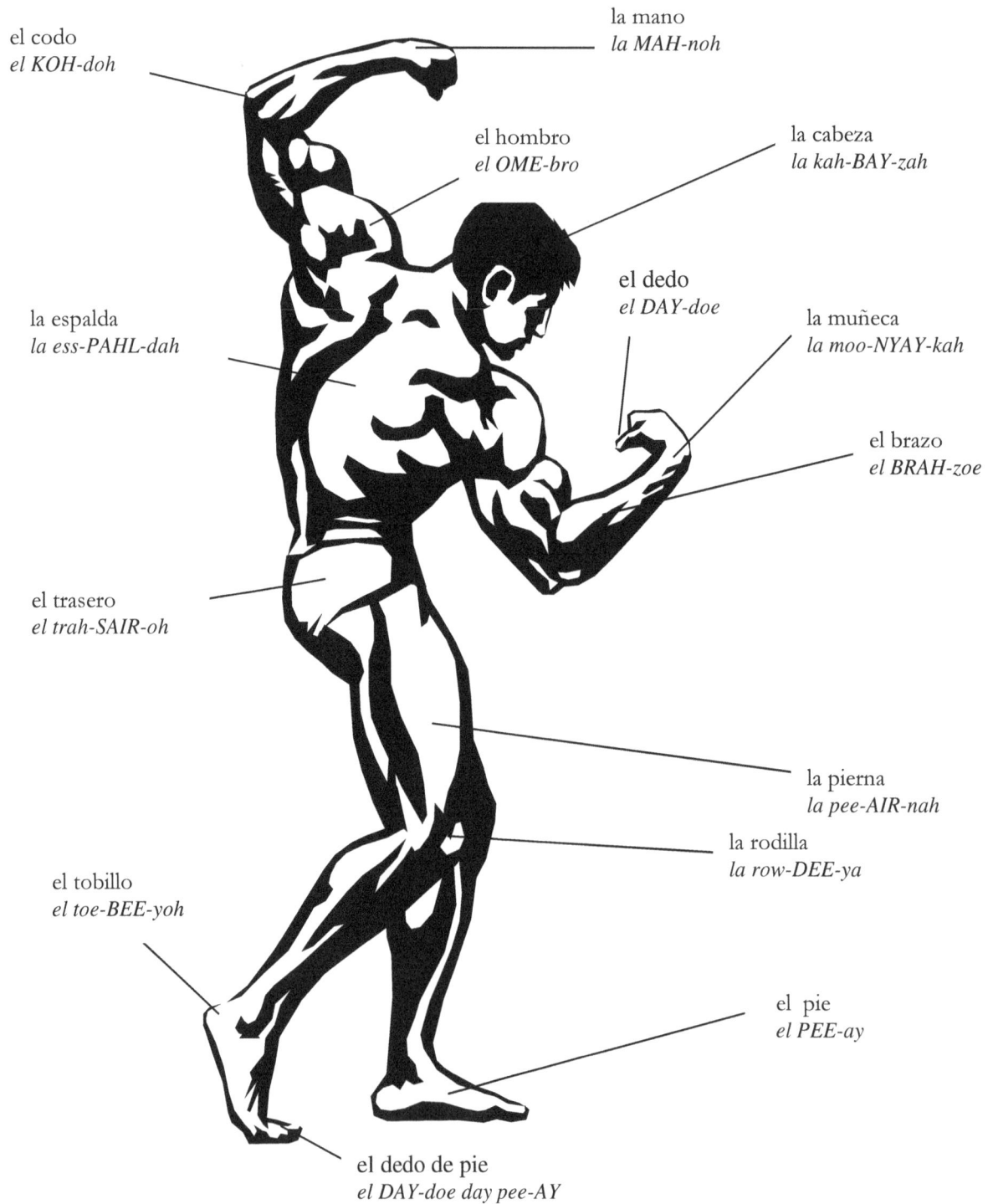

el codo
el KOH-doh

la mano
la MAH-noh

el hombro
el OME-bro

la cabeza
la kah-BAY-zah

la espalda
la ess-PAHL-dah

el dedo
el DAY-doe

la muñeca
la moo-NYAY-kah

el brazo
el BRAH-zoe

el trasero
el trah-SAIR-oh

la pierna
la pee-AIR-nah

la rodilla
la row-DEE-ya

el tobillo
el toe-BEE-yoh

el pie
el PEE-ay

el dedo de pie
el DAY-doe day pee-AY

El juego "Simón dice..."

"see-MONE say DEE-say"
(Simon Says...)

Instructions: Use the following to play "Simón dice." Remember that you MUST hear "Simón dice" before you can do the action!

ESPAÑOL	INGLÉS	EJEMPLO
toque *TOE-kay*	touch	**Toque el brazo.** *TOE-kay el BRAH-zoe*
levante *lay-BAHN-tay*	raise	**Levante la mano.** *lay-BAHN-tay la MAH-noh*
señale *sehn-YAH-lay*	point to	**Señale el pie.** *sehn-YAH-lay el pee-AY*

Actividad: Dibujar a una persona
(Draw a Person)

Instrucciones: Escuche las instrucciones y dibuje a una persona.

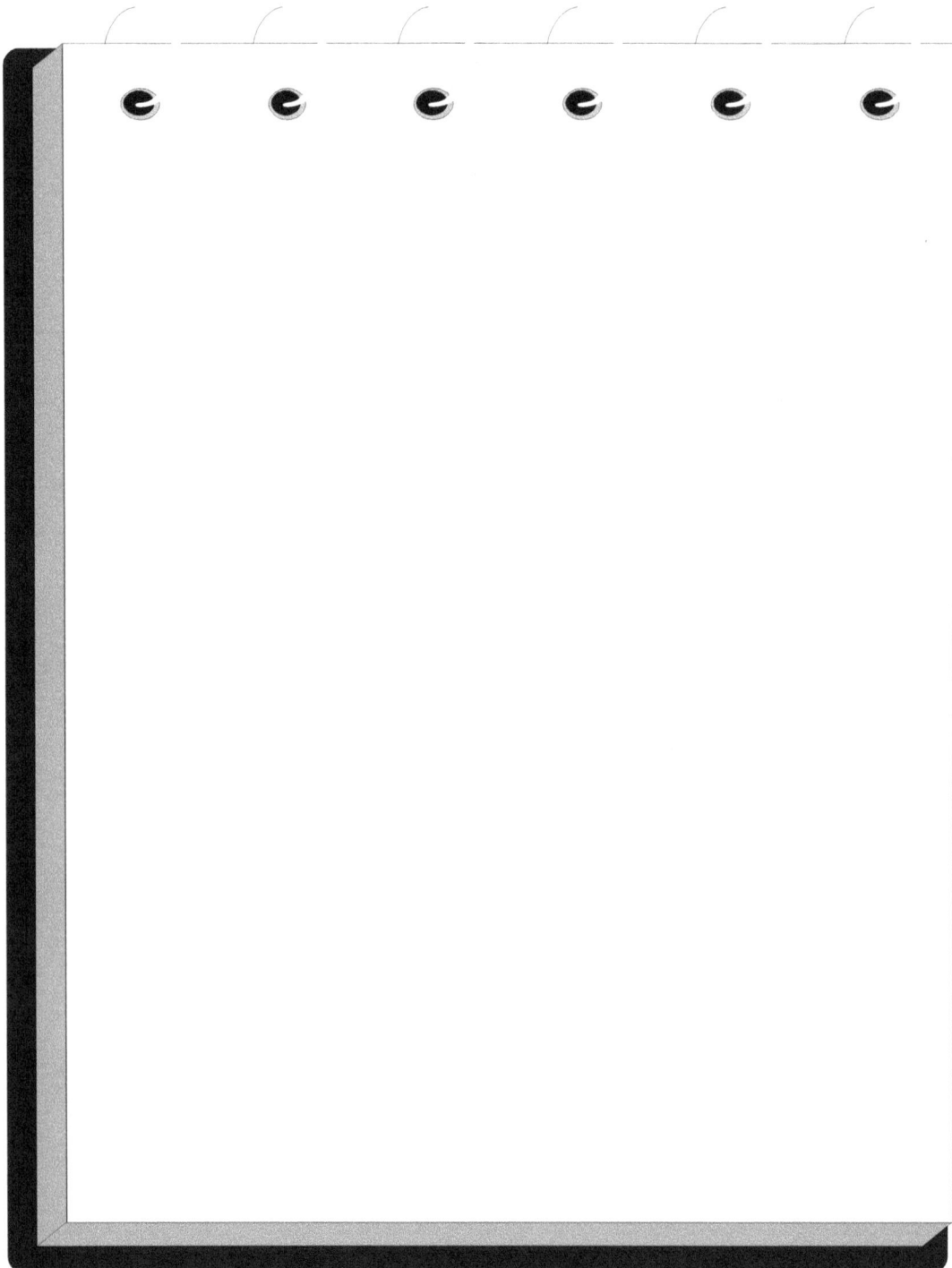

Me duele...
(My ___ hurts...)

To ask someone "What hurts?", say:

PREGUNTA: ¿Qué le duele?
kay lay DWELL-ay/ain

RESPUESTA: Me duele/n* _____ *(My ____ hurts.)*
may DWELL-ay/ain

Ó

Le duele/n _____ *(His/her _____ hurts.)*
lay DWELL-ay/ain

Ejemplos:
Médico: ¿Qué le duele?
Paciente: Me duele la cabeza.

Médico: ¿Qué le duele?
Paciente: Me duelen las piernas.

PREGUNTA ESPECÍFICA: ¿Le duele _____?

Ejemplos:
Madre: ¿Le duele la pierna?
Hijo: No, no me duele la pierna. Me duele el pie.

---

*NOTA: Use the verb "duelen" when talking about more than one body part.

For example:
Me duelen los ojos.
Me duelen los dedos.
Me duelen los pies.

93

Actividad: El médico
(The Doctor)

Instrucciones: Un paciente visita con frecuencia a su médico. En parejas, sostengan una conversación con:

Saludos *(Basic greetings)*

Preguntas sobre la familia y los amigos

El médico hace preguntas *(Ask what hurts.)*

El paciente dice cinco partes del cuerpo que le duelen *(hurts)*

El médico toma apuntes *(takes notes)* y repite qué le duele al paciente

El médico aconseja *(gives advice)* al paciente. Ejemplos:
       Tome *(take)* _____ aspirinas y llámeme mañana.
       Necesita descansar *(rest)* más.
       Necesita comer *(eat)* _____.
       Necesita *(You need to)* _____
       Hay que *(You should)* _____
       Tiene que *(You should)*_____

Emergencias

¿Qué pasó?	kay pah-SO	What happened?
¿Está herido?	ess-TAH air-EE-doh	Are you hurt?
¿Le duele?	lay DWELL-lay	Are you in pain?
¿Le duele mucho?	lay DWELL-lay MOO-cho	Does it hurt a lot?
¿Puede moverse?	PWAY-day moe-BARE-say	Can you move?
¿Necesita una ambulancia?	nehs-sess-SEE-tah OO-nah ahm-boo-LAHN-see-ah	Do you need an ambulance?
¡Llame una ambulancia!	YAH-may OO-nah ahm-boo-LAHN-see-ah	Call an ambulance!
¡Llame al nueve uno uno!	YAH-may ahl NWAY-bay OON-oh OON-oh	Call 9-1-1!
¡Llame a su familia!	YAH-may ah soo fah-MEE-lee-ah	Call his/her family!
Cálmese.	CAHL-may-say	Calm down.
No se mueva.	no say MWAY-bay	Don't move.
Estamos buscando ayuda.	ess-TAH-mohs boos-CAHN-doe ah-YOO-dah	We are looking for help.

Accidentes/Heridas comunes

ataque	ah-TAH-kay	seizure
ataque al corazón	ah-TAH-kay ahl core-ah-ZONE	heart attack
ataque por calor	ah-TAH-kay poor kah-LORE	heat stroke
brazo roto	BRAH-zoe ROW-toe	broken arm
caída grave	kie-EE-dah GRAH-bay	bad fall
congelamiento	cone-hail-ah-mee-EN-toe	frostbite
cortada seria	kor-TAH-dah SAIR-ee-ah	bad cut
derrame cerebral	day-RAH-may sair-ay-BRAHL	stroke
deshidratación	days-hee-drah-tah-see-OWN	dehydration
desmayado	days-my-AH-doe	fainted
dificultad al respirar	deef-ee-cool-TAHD ahl ray-speer-AR	breathing difficulties
dolor en el pecho	doe-LORE en el PAY-cho	chest pains
herida en la cabeza	air-EE-dah en la kah-BAY-sah	head wound
mareos	mar-AY-ohs	dizziness
pierna rota	pee-AIR-nah row-tah	broken leg
torcedura de tobillo	tore-say-DO-rah day toe-BEE-yo	sprained ankle

¡Cuidado!

kwee-DAH-doh

(Be careful!)

Does your job require safety equipment? If so, what? Draw them on the person below.

boots	**las botas**	*las BOW-tahs*	harness	**el arnés**	*el ar-NAYS*
helmet	**el casco**	*el KAHS-koh*	mask	**la máscara**	*la MAHS-car-ah*
goggles	**los anteojos**	*los ahn-tay-OH-hose*	protection for ears/eyes	**protecciróm para oídos/ojos**	*pro-tex-see-OWN PAH-rah oh-EE-dose/OH-hose*

Other Vocabulary:

96

Notas Culturales

Music & Dance

¡Felicitaciones! You made it through your Spanish class! Let's celebrate by learning about some of the more common music and dance styles in Latin America. Maybe even try a few steps!

Salsa
A generic term used to describe the mixing of a number of different styles of Latin music (such as son, cha, cha, cha, songo, timba, merengue, and rumba).
Examples: Grupo Niche, Marc Anthony

Son (Cuba)
Predates salsa-possibly the most influential style of all Latin music. Combination of African & Spanish musical elements.
Examples: Buena Vista Social Club, Arsenio Rodriguez, Trio Matamoros, Son 14

Cha cha cha (Cuba)
Cha cha cha was invented by the Cuban bandleader, Enrique Jorrin, in the 50's. Legend says it was invented because many Americans were having trouble dancing to the syncopated rhythms of traditional Cuban music.
Examples: 'Kinkamanche' by Eddie Palmieri, 'Cha Cuba' by Orquesta Aragon and 'Habana Del Este' by Afro Cuban Allstars.

Merengue (Dominican Republic)
Latin music in 2/4 time. Traditionally performed with voice, accordions, a two-headed drum called a tambora, & a hand-held metal guiro.
Examples: Juan Luis Guerra, Francisco Ulloa, La Makina, Fulanito, La Banda Gorda and Elvis Crespo

Rumba (Cuba)
The most African of styles in Cuban music. Traditionally associated with Afro-Cuban religion where a community came together to perform sacred music and dance.
Examples: Muñequitos de Matanza, Los Papines

Bachata (Dominican Republic)
Slow romantic music originally played with guitars & small percussion instruments.
Examples: Juan Luis Guerra

Cumbia (Colombia)
Cumbia is in 2/4 time and may feature instruments such as accordions, keyboards, saxophones, trumpets, trombones & a percussion section.
Examples: Lizandro Meza, Grupo Fantasma, Lucho Bermudez

Samba (Brazil)
Another broad term like Salsa which actually refers to a number of different styles. Samba is a mixture of African, European and Native American musical elements.
Examples: Martinho Da Vila, Beth Carvalho, Paulinho da Viola, Clara Nunes

Tango (Argentina)
Romantic nostalgic music-often described as the music of 'frustrated love'. Definite Spanish & European roots as well as African, Creole and Native American influences.
Examples: Carlos Gardel, Astor Piazzolla

Vallenato (Colombia)
Uses accordions, bass & percussion. Recently, has been fused with elements of rock.
Example: Carlos Vives

Tex-Mex/Ranchera (Mexico)
Best-known Mexican genre by far is ranchera, interpreted by a band called mariachi. Includes norteño and banda styles. All use the acordian as its primary instrument.
Examples: Flaco Jiménez, Selena, Tigres de Norte

Marimba (Mexico)
Southern Mexican folk music that remains popular in Chiapas and Oaxaca.
Example: Baja Marimba Band

Flamenco (Spain)
Gypsy music popular in the southern region of Andalucia. The most familiar flamenco instrument is the guitar played at a feverish and passionate pace with melodies that reflect the influence of Arabic music.
Examples: Paco de Lucia, Gypsy Kings

Appendix

- Survival Words
- Grammar (pronouns &verb tenses)

Palabras necesarias
(Survival Words)

¿Cómo se dice _____?	*KO-mo say DEE-say*	How do you say _____?
¿Qué significa _____?	*kay sig-nif-EE-ka*	What does _____ mean?
No comprendo/No entiendo.	*no comb-PREN-doe/no ehn-TYEN-doe*	I don't understand.
No sé.	*no say*	I don't know.
Repita, por favor.	*ray-PEE-tah poor fah-BOAR*	Repeat, please.
Perdón.	*pair-DOAN*	Pardon me (for an interruption)
Con permiso.	*cone pair-MEE-soh*	Pardon me (when trying to get through a crowd)

Preguntas
(Question Words)

¿Qué?	*kay*	What?
¿Cómo?	*KO-mo*	How?
¿Cuál?	*kwahl*	Which?
¿Quién?	*key-EN*	Who?
¿Por qué?	*poor KAY*	Why?
¿Cuándo?	*KWAHN-doe*	When?
¿Dónde?	*DOAN-day*	Where?
¿Cuánto?	*KWAHN-toe*	How much/many?

Verbos: 6 Verbos Comunes
(6 Common Verbs)

While there are thousands of verbs in the Spanish language, at this point we are going to focus on the most common ones to get your message across. Little by little, you will become familiar with at least dozens or maybe even hundreds more.

	PREGUNTA	RESPUESTA
Tener (to have)	¿Tiene hijos? (Do you have children?) ¿Cuántos años tiene?	• Sí, tengo hijos. • No, no tengo hijos. • Tengo 53 años.
Querer (to want)	¿Quiere sal? (Do you want salt?)	• Sí, quiero sal. • No, no quiero sal.
Necesitar (to need)	¿Necesita doctor? (Do you need a doctor?)	• Sí, necesito doctor. • No, no necesito doctor.
Haber (Is/are there? There is/are)	¿Hay un doctor aquí? (Is there a doctor here?)	• Sí, hay un doctor aquí. • No, no hay un doctor aquí.
Estar (to be) * Use with temporary conditions and location.	¿Está bien? (Are you OK?)	• Sí, estoy bien. • No, no estoy bien.
Ser (to be) * Use with everything else.	¿Es madre? (Are you a mother?)	• Sí, soy madre. • No, no soy madre.

Pronouns

		Singular		Plural
1st person	yo *(I)*		nosotros/as *(we)*	
2nd person	tú *(you informal)*		vosotros/as *(you "all" informal)*	
3rd person	él ella usted (Ud.) *(he, she, you formal)*		ellos ellas ustedes (Uds.) *(they, you, you "all" formal")*	

Grammar Forms

ESTAR – temporary condition, location

yo	estoy	nosotros/as	estamos
tú	estás	vosotros/as*	estáis*
él ella usted (Ud.)	está	ellos ellas ustedes (Uds.)	están

SER – used almost everywhere besides "temporary conditions" or "location"

yo	soy	nosotros/as	somos
tú	eres	vosotros/as*	sois*
él ella usted (Ud.)	es	ellos ellas ustedes (Uds.)	son

PRESENT TENSE

For present tense, you simply drop the last 2 letters of the verb and change it according to what the letters were. For example, if you wanted to say "I dance", change the verb "bailar" to "bailo."

	- AR	- ER	- IR		- AR	- ER	-IR
yo	-o	-o	-o	nosotros	-amos	-emos	-imos
tu	-as	-es	-es	vosotros	-áis	-éis	-ís
el, ella, ud.	-a	-e	-e	ellos, ellas,l uds.	-an	-en	-en

Present Tense Stem-Changing Verbs

(e→ie)

yo	pienso	nosotros/as	pensamos
tú	piensas	vosotros/as	pensáis
él ella usted (Ud.)	piensa	ellos ellas ustedes (Uds.)	piensan

Similar Verbs
pensar - to think
cerrar - to close
despertar - to wake up
divertirse - to have fun
empezar - to begin
encender - to turn on
hervir - to boil
mentir - to lie
perder - to lose
preferir - to prefer
querer - to want
recomendar - to recommend
sentir - to feel
sugerir- to suggest

(o→ue)

yo	puedo	nosotros/as	podemos
tú	puedes	vosotros/as	podéis
él ella usted (Ud.)	puede	ellos ellas ustedes (Uds.)	pueden

Similar Verbs
poder - to be able
acostar - to go to bed
colgar - to hang up
devolver - to give back
dormir - to sleep
encontrar - to find
mostrar - to show
probar - to try
recordar - to remember

(e→i)

yo	pido	nosotros/as	pedimos
tú	pides	vosotros/as	pedís
él ella usted (Ud.)	pide	ellos ellas ustedes (Uds.)	piden

Similar Verbs
pedir - to ask
consequir - to obtain
despedir - to say goodbye
seguir - to follow
servir - to serve
vestir - to dress

Present Progressive

This tense uses gerunds, or the "-ing" in English. You use this tense when something is happening right now—in the present moment.

Drop the last 2 letters and add:

AR verbs
- ando

ER/IR verbs
-iendo

Use the verb "estar" before the verb.

For example:
Estoy bailando.
(I am dancing.)

Está comiendo.
(He is eating.)

Estás escribiendo.
(You are writing.)

"Easy" Past Tense

To express past tense in Spanish "easily," use the "present perfect" tense. In English, this is the "to have done something" tense.

For example:
I have eaten. I have slept. I have worked.

In Spanish, use:
1) the "have" verb

He	I have	Hemos	We have
Has	You have (informal)	Habéis	You (all) have *(Spain only)*
Ha	He/She has You have (formal)	Han	They have You (all) have

2) the verb you are trying to express in the past tense. (You need to change the ending a bit, depending on if it ends in –ar, -er, or –ir.)

AR Verbs	ER Verbs	IR Verbs
bailar → bailado	comer → comido	vivir → vivido
hablar → hablado	leer → leído	ir→ ido
mirar → mirado	beber → bebido	decidir → decidido

EXAMPLES:
I have eaten. He has slept. You have worked.
He comido. Ha dormido. Ha trabajado.

"Easy" Future Tense (Ir + a + infinitive)

This is the "easy" way to express the future. We start with the verb "ir" (to go) and conjugate it as follows:

voy	I go	vamos	We go
vas	You go (informal)	vais	You (all) go *(Spain only)*
va	He/she goes You go (formal)	van	They go You (all) go

Examples:
Voy a jugar al fútbol. (I am going to play football.)
¿Vas a comer? (Are you going to eat?)

Future Tense

The future tense is quite easy as it has almost the same endings for all 3 kinds of verbs. For –ar, -er, and –ir verbs, you simply add the following to the infinitive (whole verb):

	-AR/-ER/-IR		-AR/-ER/-IR
yo	- é	nosotros	-emos
tu	- ás	vosotros	-éis
el, ella, Ud.	- á	ellos, ellas, Uds.	- án

For example:

AR Verbs

¿Bailará la salsa en la fiesta?
Will she dance the salsa at the party?

Creo que sí. Bailará salsa en la fiesta
I believe so. She will dance the salsa at the party.

ER Verbs

¿Comerá en la cafetería?
Will you eat in the cafeteria? (formal)

Sí, comeré en la cafetería.
Yes, I will eat in the cafeteria.

IR Verbs

¿Irás al cine?
Will you go to the theater? (informal)

No, no iré al cine.
No, I will not go to the theater.

Some Irregulars:
decir (dir-)
hacer (har-)
haber (habr-)
querer (querr-)
poder (podr-)
poner (pondr-)
saber (sabr-)
venir (vendr-)
tener (tendr-)

Past Tense

PAST TENSE – PRETERITE

Simply drop the last 2 letters of the verb and change it according to what the letters were. For example, if you wanted to say "I danced", change the verb "bailar" to "bailé."

	- AR	-ER/ - IR		- AR	- ER / -IR
yo	-é	-í	nosotros	-amos	-imos
tu	-aste	-iste	vosotros	-asteis	-isteis
el, ella, Ud.	-ó	-ió	ellos, ellas, Uds.	-aron	-ieron

Common irregular verbs:

Verb	Meaning	yo	tú	él, ella, Ud.	nosotros	vosotros	ellos/as, Uds.
ir/ser	to go/to be	fui	fuiste	fue	fuimos	fuisteis	fueron
dar	to give	di	diste	dio	dimos	disteis	dieron
decir	to say	dije	dijiste	dijo	dijimos	dijisteis	dijeron
estar	to be	estuve	estuviste	estuvo	estuvimos	estuvisteis	estuvieron
hacer	to do/make	hice	hiciste	hizo	hicimos	hicisteis	hicieron
poder	to be able	pude	pudiste	pudo	pudimos	pudisteis	pudieron
poner	to put	puse	pusiste	puso	pusimos	pusisteis	pusieron
tener	to have	tuve	tuviste	tuvo	tuvimos	tuvisteis	tuvieron

PAST TENSE – IMPERFECT

Simply drop the last 2 letters of the verb and add the appropriate ending. For example, if you want to say "I used to dance", change the verb "bailar" to "bailaba."

	- AR	-ER/ - IR		- AR	- ER / -IR
yo	-aba	-ía	nosotros	-ábamos	-íamos
tu	-abas	-ías	vosotros	-abais	-íais
el, ella, Ud.	-aba	-ía	ellos, ellas, Uds.	-aban	-ían

3 main irregular verb

Verb	Meaning	yo	tú	él, ella, Ud.	nosotros	vosotros	ellos/as, Uds.
ir		iba	ibas	iba	-íbamos	ibais	iban
ser		era	eras	era	éramos	erais	eran
ver		veía	veías	veía	veíamos	veías	veían

Reflexive Verbs

For these verbs, you conjugate them as you normally would, then add one of the following in front of the conjugated verb.

For example:

yo	**me** lavo	nosotros	**nos** lavamos
tu	**te** lavas	vosotros	**os** laváis
el, ella, ud.	**se** lava	ellos, ellas, uds.	**se** lavan

Otros ejemplos:
Me voy.
Te duermes.
Se cae.
Nos sentamos.
Os levantais.
Se secan.

Common "Regular" Verbs

AR VERBS				ER VERBS	
aceptar	to accept	besar	to kiss	responder	to answer
admirar	to admire	escuchar	to listen	creer	to believe
aconsejar	to advise	mirar	to look at	romper	to break
autorizar	to allow	buscar	to look for	traer* (yo traigo)	to bring
llegar	to arrive	equivocarse	to make a mistake	escoger	to choose
*estar (yo estoy)	to be	mezclar	to mix	toser	to cough
tomar	to take	llamar	to call	desaparecer	to disappear
respirar	to breathe	notar	to note	desobedecer	to disobey
cepillar	to comb	observar	to observe	beber	to drink
quemar	to burn	pintar	to paint	comer	to eat
comprar	to buy	pagar	to pay	caer* (yo caigo)	to fall
llamar	to call	organizar	to organize	suceder	to happen
calmar	to calm	preparar	to prepare	tener*	to have
verificar	to check	presentar	to present	conocer* (yo conozco)	to know
peinar	to comb	castigar	to punish		
entrar	to come in	empujar	to push	aprender	to learn
comparar	to compare	alquilar	to rent	deber	to must
continuar	to continue	reservar	to reserve	obedecer	to obey
llorar	to cry	descansar	to rest	ofrecer* (yo ofrezco)	to offer
cortar	to cut	enviar	to envy	prometer	to promise
detestar	to detest	separar	to seperate	poner* (yo pongo)	to put
divorciar	to divorce	quedar	to stay	leer	to read
dibujar	to draw	estudiar	to study	reconocer* (yo reconozco)	to recognize
secar	to dry off	lograr	to earn		
borrar	to erase	nadar	to swim	parecer	to seem
examinar	to examine	tomar	to take	vender	to sell
explicar	to explain	pasear	to take a walk		
llenar	to fill	hablar	to talk	IR VERBS	
acabar	to finish	echar	to throw	asistir a	to attend
olvidar	to forget	delinear	to trace	describir	to discover
engordar	to gain weight	viajar	to travel	destruir	to destroy
levantarse	to lift	apagar	to turn off	ir*	to go
dar	to give	esperar	to wait	salir* (yo salgo)	to go out
regresar	to go back	caminar	to walk	subir	to go up
odiar	to hate	lavar	to wash	abrir	to open
calentar	to heat	mirar	to watch	decir* (yo digo)	to say
esperar	to hope	llevar	to wear	servir	to serve
identificar	to identify	secar	to dry	compartir	to share
informar	to inform	preocupar	to worry	sugerir	to suggest
invitar	to invite	gritar	to yell	escribir	to write
				vivir	to live

About Pronto Spanish™

At Pronto Spanish, we believe that:

- People can learn another language efficiently and effectively in an enjoyable, relaxed, and low-key atmosphere.

- Communication among people is the key to peace and harmony in neighborhoods, in the workplace and beyond. Language barriers can and should be broken down.

- All people, regardless of national origin, sex, gender, race, orientation or ethnicity, deserve to be treated with respect and dignity and at all times.

To learn more about our **on-line Occupational Spanish courses** or other products below, please visit our website at www.prontospanish.com.

Title	ISBN 13
¡A Trabajar! A Guide to Occupational Spanish Instructor's Guide	978-1-934467-01-5
Spanish for Banking Pronto Guide™ & Audio CD	978-1-934467-21-3
Spanish for Construction Pronto Guide™ & Audio CD	978-1-934467-02-2
Spanish for Educators Pronto Guide™ & Audio CD	978-1-934467-03-9
Spanish for Food Service Pronto Guide™ & Audio CD	978-1-934467-06-0
Spanish for Health Care Pronto Guide™ & Audio CD	978-1-934467-07-7
Spanish for Hospitality Pronto Guide™ & Audio CD	978-1-934467-05-3
Spanish for Human Resources Pronto Guide™ & Audio CD	978-1-934467-04-6
Spanish for Law Enforcement Pronto Guide™ & Audio CD	978-1-934467-23-7
Spanish for Manufacturing Pronto Guide™ & Audio CD	978-1-934467-22-0
Spanish for Social Work Pronto Guide™ & Audio CD	978-1-934467-28-2
¡A Conversar! 1 Student Workbook w/Audio CD	978-0-9777727-0-4
¡A Conversar! 2 Student Workbook w/Audio CD	978-0-9777727-2-8
¡A Conversar! 3 Student Workbook w/Audio CD	978-0-9777727-4-2
¡A Conversar! 4 Student Workbook w/Audio CD	978-0-9777727-6-6

About the Author

Tara Bradley Williams, founder of **Pronto Spanish™** and author of the **¡A Trabajar!** and **¡A Conversar!** series has many years of Spanish teaching experience at the high school and community college levels. Through her teaching, she found that many students simply wanted to learn Spanish in an enjoyable way in order to communicate on a basic level without having to learn grammar rules taught in a traditional academic setting. Pronto Spanish, ¡A Trabajar! and ¡A Conversar! were created just for these people.

Tara has a BA degree in Spanish and Sociology from St. Norbert College and a MA in Higher Education and Adult Studies from the University of Denver. She has studied Spanish at the Universidad de Ortega y Gasset, in Toledo, Spain and has lived and traveled extensively in Spain and Latin America. Tara currently lives in Wisconsin with her husband and three children.

www.ingramcontent.com/pod-product-compliance
Lightning Source LLC
Chambersburg PA
CBHW080520110426
42742CB00017B/3185